SIMPLE CHINESE COOKING

For Indy, Jyesy and Finny

Kylie Kwong

Simple Chinese Cooking

with photography by Earl Carter

Viking Studio

CONTENTS

EQUIPMENT FOR THE CHINESE KITCHEN

WOKS

'Wok' is the Cantonese word for pot – which should give you an idea of the central place this simple utensil occupies in the Chinese kitchen.

There are various-shaped woks available, fashioned out of different materials and designed for different heat sources. The traditional round-bottomed wok is designed for cooking over an open flame, such as a gas stove – the round wok sides hugged by the flames act as the perfect heat conductor. Flat-bottomed woks are specifically designed for electric stoves – although the experience doesn't really compare with the excitement of cooking over a raw flame, the rounded sides are still sympathetic with the motions of stir-frying. Moreover, a flat-bottomed wok never topples over! Whether cooking with gas or electricity, the most important thing when stir-frying is to ensure that as much of the wok's surface area as possible is in contact with the heat source, so you get the intense heat necessary.

Then there is the electric wok – simply plug into a power point and away you go! I am very impressed by electric woks these days: contrary to popular opinion, they *do* reach temperatures hot enough to successfully sear a scallop, a fillet of fish or a sliver of chicken. Electric woks are also brilliant for Chinese-style steaming. They are readily available and quite affordable; their non-stick surface means they don't need to be seasoned like carbon-steel woks (see below), and also makes them easy to clean.

You can buy steel woks in all Chinese supermarkets. They are inexpensive and last for a very long time – the only thing to look out for when you buy a wok is that it fits your gas ring or electric coil. 'Wok lids' are bought separately; I love the really sweet, bright-red ones in Chinatown, which I always buy because red symbolises luck and prosperity for the Chinese. Or you can use an ordinary saucepan lid, as long as it fits snugly within the top half of the wok.

To prepare, or season, a new steel wok, use warm soapy water and a non-stainless-steel scourer to scrub off the greasy film which coats the wok. Dry thoroughly then pour some oil onto a paper towel and give the wok a good once-over. This should be done after each time you use the wok, to ensure rust prevention. Over time, as you use the wok, it will turn black, and eventually will take on a dense black colour to become a 'well-seasoned' wok. If treated with care, you can have a wok for years! A well-seasoned wok is a source of great pride among the Chinese, infused as it is with lots of beautiful food memories and stories that have become ingrained in its patina.

Cooking utensils to use when stir-frying in your wok include chopsticks, wooden or metal spoons and spatulas, tongs – whatever you feel comfy with and is appropriate to the surface of the wok. Obviously, in the case of an electric wok, with its Teflon surface, take care to use only wooden or plastic implements.

If you do not have a wok, a shallow non-stick frypan will suffice for stir-frying.

STEAMERS

I think the Chinese way of steaming is brilliantly simple – a lidded basket set over a pan of boiling water. There are two types of steaming vessels, bamboo and aluminium. Both are inexpensive and work very well, so it really comes down to personal preference.

Most of us are familiar with the traditional, visually appealing bamboo steamers hand-fashioned from woven bamboo. The slightly dome-shaped lid absorbs any condensation, so that no liquid drips down to waterlog the food. Bamboo steamers are sold with one lid and as many tiers of baskets as you like – or as will fit in your kitchen . . . Look out for steamers with 'woven' lacings or 'ties' along the side, as these equate to a strong, firm basket. With repeated use, the bamboo inevitably wears and weakens, so it helps to buy a well-made one initially – mind you, bamboo steamers are so cheap, it's not really worth losing sleep over.

In my restaurant I use aluminium steamers for their longer shelf-life – the work-out a restaurant's steaming equipment endures each day, compared to a domestic situation, is enormous. The other advantage of the aluminium version is that it comes with a perfectly-fitting pan to hold the boiling water, whereas the bamboo steamer relies on the cook to choose a pan that suits its dimensions. On the other hand, I use a bamboo steamer at home purely for aesthetic reasons – I just love the arty, traditional, rustic look. When I'm not using my bamboo steamer I hang it up on the wall, where it becomes a piece of 'kitchen art'!

I could not live without my bamboo steamer – and not just for cooking Chinese food. As well as steaming any vegetables and fish to perfection, they are also excellent for reheating food, keeping rice hot, and for warming bowls and plates prior to serving a meal. They are so easy to clean (just use warm soapy water and a non-steel scourer) and so simple to store – hang them on a nail or hook in your kitchen, or neatly stack the baskets and lids. They are light in weight and low in price, so you can afford to buy a range of sizes suitable for cooking anything from a small fish fillet or a handful of dumplings to a plate-size snapper or a whole chicken or duck.

Both types of steamer are readily available at all Chinese supermarkets and some regular supermarkets, as well as in kitchenware shops.

UTENSILS

Alongside the usual array of tongs, spatulas, metal spoons, wooden spoons, ladles, measuring cups and jugs, scales, paring knives, vegetable peelers, preparation bowls, a range of small to large saucepans, one or two 10-litre (10-quart) stockpots with lids, I would advise you to consider the following tools to complete your Chinese kitchen:

> medium-sized mesh **strainer/sieve** – approximately 10 centimetres (4 inches) diameter – required for fine work such as straining chilli flakes from oil.

> large **chef's** pair of **wooden chopsticks** – these are very practical, especially when retrieving an ingredient from a wok filled with deep-frying oil; their length makes them safer, as long as you are a reasonably confident chopstick-er!

> shallow brass medium-sized **basket** or stainless-steel **'spider'** – approximately 12 centimetres (5 inches) diameter – for scooping and draining.

> **mortar and pestle**, preferably granite (I do not use food processors in my Chinese cooking); I find the porcelain or clay versions too fragile for regular use. The granite ones are brilliant because of their density and weight, which means they can take years of intense grinding and pounding. They come in several sizes, but I suggest you buy one at least 16 centimetres (6 inches) diameter.

> **Chinese cleaver** – great for chopping through chicken and duck bones! Buy a cleaver as you would a regular chef's knife: ensure that the grip feels comfortable and is the right size for your hand, and that the 'weight' of the knife is appropriate for you. These two factors will directly affect the deftness with which you use the cleaver. I prefer the wooden-handled cleavers as the metal-handled ones become slippery all too easily if your hands are wet or have food on them.

> **cartouche** – a French term for a piece of paper used to cover the surface of poaching or braising food. The paper reduces evaporation and skinning of the liquid, as well as helping to keep the food submerged so that it cooks evenly. The French have a very sophisticated and correct way of creating a cartouche, which looks a little like origami! For the purposes of the recipes in this book, just tear a piece of baking paper or greaseproof paper to roughly the size and shape of your pan and ensure that it covers the ingredients in the liquid.

> **muslin** – a fine cotton cloth used by chefs to finely strain stocks and sauces. It is available at speciality kitchenware outlets and some fabric shops, but I find that a clean Chux or J-Cloth works just as well.

INGREDIENTS

Every recipe in this book celebrates freshness and, of course, encourages buying food that is in season and therefore at its best and most bountiful.

BLACK CLOUD EAR FUNGUS

Grown in southern New South Wales, this fungus boasts a beautiful, black, velvety-smooth texture, is crunchy and refreshing when served raw in salads, as well as excellent for any type of cooking method. Black cloud ear fungus is also available dried, but I prefer the fresh, which is increasingly available in supermarkets.

BOK CHOY

One of the most popular, versatile and well-known Chinese leafy vegetables, bok choy is available year-round. It has snow-white or light-green stalks, a slightly bulbous base and green leaves with a mild, refreshing, tangy flavour.

BROWN SUGAR

Although this is just white sugar that has had clarified molasses added to it, I like its caramelly flavour.

CASSIA BARK

This is like a more intense version of cinnamon. It is the thick, inner bark of an evergreen of the laurel family that's native to China, and has a ruddier brown colour than cinnamon, with a pungent smell. Cassia bark is generally available in Chinese supermarkets, but substitute cinnamon quills if you can't find it.

CHILLIES

Chillies in Chinese cuisine are strongly associated with the fiery, spicy fare of Sichuan province, in south-western China. Interestingly enough, my Cantonese mother rarely cooked with chillies, but I have since become addicted to them! I use long red and green chillies a lot in my cooking: they are sweet and have a medium heat. In general, the smaller a chilli the hotter it is, and the seeds are the hottest part – so if you want less heat, deseed chillies before using them. For my recipes, it's really up to you and your taste buds how many chillies you add!

CHILLI FLAKES

These are simply fresh chillies that have been left in the sun to dry and then pounded into flakes. The drying process intensifies the flavour, making dried chilli flakes flavourful and sweet as well as fiery. These qualities are particularly useful when creating chilli sauces or oils: to make chilli oil, add a tablespoon of chilli flakes to half a cup of vegetable oil in a wok, heat gently for a few minutes, allow to cool, then strain the oil. What you have left is this delicious, bright orange oil with a mysterious and smoky note. Chilli oil will keep in the fridge for several months.

CHILLI OIL

Also called hot oil or red pepper oil, these bottles of ready-made chilli oil pack a punch. I like using it in dressings and stir-fries to give the dish a bit of a kick!

CHILLI POWDER

This is simply dried chillies that have been ground to a fine powder; it is essential for making chilli-salt, and is also great for adding to spice pastes.

CHINESE BBQ SAUCE

This sauce is made from soy beans, salt, sugar, garlic, pepper and Chinese five-spice powder. Its sticky, luscious consistency and rich, dark browny-red hue make it excellent for marinating meats.

CHINESE WHITE CABBAGE

With an oblong head 15–25 centimetres (6–10 inches long), this cabbage has a light, sweet, delicate flavour and a crunchy texture. It can be served raw, shredded and tossed in salads, or steamed, stir-fried or braised. It is also often called Shanghai cabbage or wonga buk.

CHOY SUM

This green leafy vegetable has narrow stems and oval leaves, and is full of yellow flowers. It is bitter, with a mustard-like tang, and is delicious stir-fried, blanched or steamed.

CINNAMON QUILLS

Cinnamon adds a robust taste to dishes. It is an essential component of five-spice powder and of the 'master' stock used in red-cooking.

CORNFLOUR

Cornflour or cornstarch is used to create that essential crunchy coating in dishes such as sweet and sour pork. In traditional Chinese cuisine, it is also often used to thicken sauces because it thickens with a clear sheen, as opposed to flour, which produces a more cloudy sauce. However, I very rarely use cornflour for this purpose, preferring to allow the natural juices and sauces of a dish to speak for themselves.

EGGS

Always buy free-range organic eggs if at all possible – the difference in flavour between a naturally farmed egg and a commercially farmed egg is incomparable, not to mention a healthier option. Check the use-by dates on egg cartons in the supermarkets; a quick way to gauge freshness is to pick one up – a fresh egg should feel heavy in your hand and have a clean smell. Store eggs in the fridge within their carton.

EXTRA VIRGIN OLIVE OIL

I know it is slightly unusual to add olive oil to Chinese food, but because I love the fruity flavour and intense yellow–green colour of extra virgin olive oil so much I just can't resist sneaking it into my salad dressings!

FISH AND SEAFOOD

The one thing I will say about seafood is 'It must be eaten fresh!' With this mantra in mind, always try to purchase seafood on the day you will eat it or, at a stretch, the day before. Seafood and fish must be refrigerated as soon after purchase as possible – if practical, keep a small esky in the car for this purpose.

When buying whole fish, choose fish that does *not* smell 'fishy' and has a natural kind of 'glow' and sheen to the body. It should be light pink inside the gills, with clear protruding eyes and have a gut with no yellowy-brown tinges and firm-textured flesh as opposed to mushy flesh.

Never buy fish fillets that have a fishy smell (fresh fish does not smell!) or are grey, yellowy or brownish in colour; fresh fish fillets should be either pure white or have a soft pink hue. They should not be sitting on mounds of ice either, as ice burns the flesh, making it soggy. Fresh fish fillets will have a slightly oily look as well, pointing to the fact that they have not been under ice or water and have not been frozen. If you wish, you can purchase a whole fish and ask the fishmonger to fillet it for you on the spot – this way, you will know that the fillets will be in great shape.

See also Prawns; Squid and calamari.

FISH SAUCE

This clear, amber-coloured liquid is the product of salted and fermented fish. It has a unique, pungent taste and an aroma that are irreplaceable. It is one of my favourite seasonings – I use it in stir-fries, marinades, braises, salad dressings and dipping sauces. Reliable brands include Squid and Golden Boy.

FIVE-SPICE POWDER

A variable mixture of 5–7 spices – cinnamon, star anise, fennel seed, cloves, liquorice root, Sichuan peppercorns, ground ginger – make up this exotic mix that is used in marinades and braises. Buy ready-ground and, like any dried spice, store in an airtight container away from light, heat and moisture.

GAI CHOY

Also known as mustard cabbage, this vegetable is deep green with a bulbous core and thick, curved stems that bear coarse, wrinkly leaves. It has a tangy, bitter flavour and is great for stir-frying, braising and serving in soups.

GARLIC

This has been integral to the food and medicine of East Asia for thousands of years – in fact, East Asians boast the world's highest per-capita garlic consumption! I particularly love simple but scrumptious stir-fries of Chinese vegetables tossed with salt and lashings of garlic. Garlic should be used within an hour or less of being prepared, whether minced, diced or crushed. Never, ever use bottled minced garlic (it is filled with preservatives and tastes artificial and dreadful) or dried, powdered garlic. Always purchase the firmest heads of garlic – firmness is an indication of freshness.

GINGER

Fresh ginger, with its clean, aromatic flavour, is a mainstay of Chinese cuisine – especially in combination with spring onions and soy sauce. Always choose the firmest, heaviest roots with smooth, taut skin, and avoid any wrinkled-

slippery texture. They are brilliant for stir-frying, steaming and adding to soups. Dick Ap is my preferred brand, but there are plenty of others to choose from.

RICE WINE VINEGAR

This is made from rice wine lees and alcohol. I like the soft, round, balanced flavour of Japanese brand Mitsukan, but any type of white or malt vinegar can be used as a substitute when cooking recipes from this book.

SALAD VEGETABLES AND HERBS

When I use lettuces and herbs in my Chinese cooking, I mostly use them raw, so it is imperative that they are the freshest available. Take time to touch, look and smell the various bunches on the refrigerated shelves – don't be embarrassed about foraging for the fresher bunch at the back! After all, there is nothing wrong with demanding fresh, quality produce. Look for intensely coloured salad vegetables and herbs, and check for brown-tinged slimy leaves or any signs of caterpillar infestation. Again, whenever possible, I urge you to buy chemical- and pesticide-free produce. Because the flavour of such produce is much more intense, you only need to purchase small amounts . . . what counts is quality, not quantity.

SALTED BLACK BEANS

Also known as fermented black beans, these small soy beans are preserved by fermentation with salt and spices, which gives them their distinctive salty, rich taste and pungent smell. They are frequently used in conjunction with ginger and garlic, and have a particular affinity with seafood and rich meats. Some people insist on rinsing black beans before use, but I never do. Double Rings is a good brand.

SEA SALT

Salt brings out the natural flavours in food and also draws out its moisture. I use sea salt – simply evaporated sea water – for its purity and natural flavour, as well as its flaky texture. Many table and kitchen salts are over-refined and adulterated with anti-caking agents and the like – try to find Maldon or Murray River salt flakes.

SESAME OIL

This amber-coloured oil is pressed from roasted sesame seeds. Used in small quantities so as not to overwhelm the subtleties of a dish, sesame oil adds an aromatic, nutty taste that enhances other flavours. Kinlan, Yeo's, Dynasty and Kodaya are all reliable brands.

SESAME SEEDS

Both white and black sesame seeds are a common garnish in Chinese cuisine, prized for their colour, taste and crunch. Called 'foreign hemp' by the Chinese, sesame seeds should be dry-roasted before use to bring out their flavour.

SHAO HSING WINE

This is the staple cooking wine in China, where it has been made in the south-western province of Zheijiang for over 2000 years. A blend of glutinous rice, rice millet, yeast and water, it is aged in earthenware vessels for about 10 years in underground cellars. Its rich, mellow taste enhances stir-fries, braises and stocks; like any alcohol, shao hsing deepens, broadens, sweetens and softens dishes, adding complexity of flavour. My favourite brand is Pagoda Blue Label Shao Hsing Huia Tiao Chew Brand, but dry sherry can also be used (see below).

SHERRY

Like many traditional Chinese cooks, my mother uses dry sherry instead of shao hsing wine (see above); it has similar properties and makes a fine substitute.

SICHUAN PEPPER AND SALT *(see opposite)*

This mixture is used to sprinkle over or through stir-fries, salads, braises and so on.

    1 tablespoon Sichuan peppercorns
    3 tablespoons sea salt

Dry-roast peppercorns and salt in a heavy-based pan. When the peppercorns begin to 'pop' and become aromatic, take off the heat. Allow to cool, then grind to a powder in a mortar and pestle or spice grinder.
(Makes 4 tablespoons; store in an airtight container.)

SICHUAN PEPPERCORNS

These hollow, reddish-brown 'peppercorns' are actually the dried berries of the prickly ash tree. They are intensely aromatic with a charming woody fragrance, and should always be dry-roasted before use to bring out all their aromatic oils. When eaten they leave a pleasantly numbing, tingly sensation on your tongue, which some find addictive – I can't live without them!

SOY SAUCE

This naturally fermented product is made from roasted soybean meal and usually wheat, and then aged for up to two years. Dark soy sauce is aged longer than light soy sauce and mixed with molasses, which gives it that dark, caramel colour. Light soy sauce is used in dressings, stir-fries, braises and steamed dishes while dark soy sauce is better for marinades, stocks and braises. Some inferior versions are full of chemicals, so make sure you buy naturally fermented soy sauce: reliable brands of light soy sauce include Kikkoman, Pearl River Bridge and Healthy Boy Yellow Label; and Pearl River Bridge or Pun Chun Premium for dark soy sauces.

    See also Tamari.

SQUID AND CALAMARI

Because most of us are time-poor, it is tempting to buy ready-cleaned squid and calamari tubes, since cleaning and preparing them from scratch can be fiddly and rather messy. Most of the time, the tubes have been frozen and then thawed ready for sale, so the natural flavour is somewhat diminished, but because squid and calamari tend to be revered mainly for their texture, I do still use the frozen version if fresh is not an option. Fresh squid and calamari should smell sweet with no trace of ammonia (which is sometimes used in the processing). Squid and calamari should be used soon after purchase and, because they readily absorb water, should never be left sitting in water or ice for long periods of time.

STAR ANISE

The hard, star-shaped, eight-pointed seed pod from a member of the magnolia family, star anise has an extremely robust, liquorice-like flavour and scent. It is used in traditional Chinese stocks and braises, usually with soy sauce and cinnamon, and is an essential ingredient in five-spice powder. Its pretty and unusual appearance makes it a beautiful garnish as well.

SUGAR *see* Brown sugar; White sugar

TAMARI

Tamari is a rich, dark soy sauce brewed without wheat. I particularly like the Spiral brand, as it is organic and has a beautifully, clean, round flavour.

TOFU

Also known as bean cake, soybean cheese and bean curd, tofu is a protein-rich, low-fat food made from soy milk coagulated using either natural gypsum or nigari, which is derived from seawater.

    Tofu has a distinctive smooth, silky, velvety texture and a rather neutral, bland taste; like mushrooms, it is a wonderful vehicle for flavour. Tofu is an excellent and very versatile food – especially for vegetarians – and can be steamed, braised, stir-fried or deep-fried.

    The compression time of the bean curd determines its 'firmness'. Silken tofu has a short compression time, while firm tofu is compressed for the longest time. Five-spice pressed tofu is also a firm-textured tofu, but is pale-brown in colour from being braised in dark soy sauce during its preparation.

    When buying tofu, always check the use-by date. There is nothing worse than tofu that has gone off: it takes on a rather unpleasant odour, and sometimes a yellowy-green slime appears on the tofu. Another warning sign is a 'bloated' packet that feels as though it is about to explode – this indicates that the tofu is fermenting. My favourite brands are Soya King silken tofu and Unigreen '5 Spice Bean Cake' pressed tofu.

VEGETABLE OIL

Cottonseed, canola, soybean, safflower and sunflower oils are perfect for deep-frying as they have a neutral, unobtrusive flavour and odour.

VEGETABLES

When choosing vegetables, always go for the most firm-skinned and tender young ones that are vibrant-coloured, intense and fresh-smelling. Obviously, you should avoid any vegetables that show signs of wilting or browning, are caterpillar-affected, fibrous or gnarly. Even when buying unusual vegetables that you may be unfamiliar with, these simple rules apply.

See also Salad vegetables and herbs.

VINEGAR *see* Malt vinegar; White vinegar

WHITE PEPPERCORNS

I tend to use white peppercorns instead of black peppercorns because they are hotter and less aromatic. When garnishing dishes with ground white pepper, be sure to sprinkle only a small pinch, as it can be overpowering.

WHITE SUGAR

The Chinese use white sugar extensively in stir-fries and dipping sauces.

WHITE VINEGAR

I use this vinegar to make pickles, and in sweet and sour sauce. Although it is rather sweet and harsh, when simmered the flavour seems to lengthen out – and in these dishes I want the sour, vinegary note to leap out at you.

WONTON WRAPPERS

Usually 7 centimetres (3 inches) square, but sometimes round, these are available in the refrigerated sections of most supermarkets in 250-gram (8-ounce) packets. I think there is little difference between the various brands; I always buy the yellow wonton wrappers that are made from eggs, flour and water, but the white ones made from just flour and water are equally good. Always check the use-by date, and reject any wrappers with dark mouldy spots visible through the packaging!

Wonton wrappers are useful not only for making wontons, but are also great simply fried in a little bit of vegetable oil – they puff up like crisps and go beautifully with a bowl of Chinese-style pickles.

stocks

Light Chinese Chicken Stock

Makes about 14 cups

I love Chinese stocks because they are very light and fresh; they do not call for extended hours of simmering. This stock is delicious as a simple soup base and is great for adding to stir-fries or braises. Always keep some handy in the freezer, especially if you are pressed for time. A stock can be easily transformed into the most incredible soup in a matter of minutes.

2 kg (4 lb) free-range chicken carcasses,
    wings and bones
6 litres (6 quarts) cold water
16 spring onions (scallions), trimmed
    and cut in half crossways

1 large red onion, roughly chopped
10 slices ginger
10 garlic cloves, crushed

Place chicken pieces in a large stockpot with remaining ingredients and bring to the boil. Reduce heat to a gentle simmer, skimming the surface with a ladle to remove any impurities.

Turn down heat until surface of the stock is barely moving and cook for 2 hours, skimming as required.

Remove stock from stove and discard chicken carcasses, wings and bones. Strain stock through muslin (or a clean Chux or J-Cloth) and store, covered, in the refrigerator for up to 3 days or in the freezer for 2–3 months.

Rich Chinese Chicken Stock

Makes about 10 cups

By using a whole chicken you can create a deep, richly flavoured and textured stock that is perfect for a hearty winter's soup. I always remind my staff that the key to good stock-making is having the best-quality ingredients. Stocks influence so many dishes; it is as if a little of their 'spirit' is being released into each dish they touch, whether it be a soup or a stir-fry. Quality is of the utmost importance.

1 × 1.8 kg (3 lb 10 oz) free-range chicken
4 litres (4 quarts) cold water
10 spring onions (scallions), trimmed
  and cut in half crossways

1 large red onion, roughly chopped
10 slices ginger
10 garlic cloves, crushed

Rinse chicken and trim away excess fat from inside and outside cavity. Cut chicken into about 10 pieces and place in a large stockpot, along with all the remaining ingredients. Bring to the boil, then reduce heat to a gentle simmer, skimming the surface with a ladle to remove any impurities.

Turn down heat until surface of the stock is barely moving and cook for 2 hours, skimming as required.

Remove stock from stove and discard chicken pieces. Strain stock through muslin (or a clean Chux or J-Cloth) and store, covered, in the refrigerator for up to 3 days or in the freezer for 2–3 months.

Chinese Fish Stock

Makes about 8 cups

I like the subtlety of fish, and this stock is beautiful, delicate and refined. I prefer to use sweet-flavoured, white-fleshed, delicate fish for this stock, such as snapper, bream, flathead, perch, sea bass, halibut and cod. I find that oily fish like mackerel, herring and sardine can be far too overpowering for stock. Ask your fishmonger for some fresh fish carcasses to make this stock.

600 g (1 lb 4 oz) fresh fish carcasses, heads and tails
3 litres (3 quarts) cold water
6 spring onions (scallions), trimmed and cut into 5 cm (2 in) lengths

1 small white onion, finely diced
½ cup finely sliced coriander (cilantro) roots and stems
10 slices ginger
5 garlic cloves, crushed

Wash fish carcass, heads and tails well under cold running water. Place all ingredients in a large stockpot and bring to the boil. Reduce heat to a gentle simmer, skimming the surface with a ladle to remove any impurities.

Turn down heat until surface of the stock is barely moving and cook for 30 minutes, skimming as required.

Remove stock from stove and discard fish carcasses, heads and tails. Strain stock through muslin (or a clean Chux or J-Cloth) and store, covered, in the refrigerator for up to 2 days or in the freezer for 1 month.

Chinese Vegetable Stock

Makes about 12–15 cups

Gently sautéing the vegetables with sea salt helps to bring out their natural flavours and colours. By using the freshest vegetables, you can create a stock that is full of vibrancy and life. This stock is great to have in the freezer: it is excellent as a soup base and adds depth of flavour to stir-fries.

1 tablespoon vegetable oil
2 medium-sized red onions, finely diced
15 slices ginger
10 garlic cloves, crushed
1 tablespoon sea salt
3 medium-sized carrots, peeled and sliced

6 sticks of celery, sliced
10 spring onions (scallions), trimmed
    and cut into 5 cm (2 in) lengths
¾ cup finely sliced coriander (cilantro)
    roots and stems
6 litres (6 quarts) cold water

Heat oil in a large stockpot, add onions, ginger, garlic and salt, and sauté over high heat for 1 minute. Add carrots, celery, spring onions and coriander, reduce heat and sauté, stirring often, for a further 3 minutes or until vegetables are very lightly browned.

Add water to the pot and bring to the boil. Reduce heat to a gentle simmer, skimming the surface with a ladle to remove any impurities.

Turn down heat until surface of the stock is barely moving and cook for 1 hour, skimming as required.

Remove stock from stove, strain through muslin (or a clean Chux or J-Cloth) and store, covered, in the refrigerator for up to 3 days or in the freezer for 2–3 months.

soups

Sweet Corn Soup

Serve as a starter for 4

This classic Chinese soup is transformed into a mouth-watering experience simply buy using fresh corn instead of creamed corn out of a tin. Many traditional recipes use cornflour as a thickening agent, but I like to keep it natural. The addition of eggs in the final stages of cooking creates a ribboning effect that subtly thickens the soup, and the combination of crunchy, sweet corn kernels and fluffy, gelatinous eggs works perfectly.

4 cobs sweet corn
2 tablespoons vegetable oil
1 small white onion, finely diced
2 tablespoons ginger julienne
1 garlic clove, finely diced
1 teaspoon sea salt

½ cup shao hsing wine or dry sherry
7 cups Light Chinese Chicken Stock (page 21)
1½ teaspoons light soy sauce
2 eggs, lightly beaten
1 tablespoon finely sliced spring onions
   (scallions)

Remove kernels from corn cobs by running a sharp knife down the sides of each cob – you should have about 3 cups of corn kernels.

Heat oil in a medium-sized heavy-based pot and sauté onion, ginger, garlic and salt for 1 minute. Add wine or sherry and simmer for a further minute or until liquid has reduced by half. Stir in corn and stock and bring to the boil. Reduce heat and simmer gently for 30 minutes. During the cooking time you may need to skim the surface of the soup occasionally to remove any impurities.

Stir through soy sauce. Lower heat and slowly pour beaten egg into soup in a thin stream, stirring constantly with a fork. Remove soup from stove as soon as you see the egg forming fine 'ribbons'.

Serve soup in bowls and garnish with spring onions.

Sweet Corn and Chicken Soup

Serve as a starter for 4

4 cobs sweet corn

1 small white onion

1 garlic clove

5 cm (2 in) knob ginger

2 tablespoons vegetable oil

1 teaspoon sea salt

½ cup shao hsing wine or dry sherry

7 cups Light Chinese Chicken Stock
(page 21)

200 g (6½ oz) free-range chicken
breast, cut widthways into
1 cm (½ in) slices

2 teaspoons light soy sauce

2 eggs, lightly beaten

1 tablespoon finely sliced
spring onions (scallions)

This peasant-style soup is a favourite in the Kwong household. The thinly sliced strips of chicken are gently poached in the soup, so they remain moist and tender. The addition of shao hsing wine or dry sherry intensifies and deepens the overall flavour and complexity.

1 Remove kernels from corn cobs by running a sharp knife down the sides of each cob – you should have about 3 cups of corn kernels. Peel and finely dice onion and garlic. Peel ginger and cut into thin slices and then into fine strips (julienne) – you should have about 2 tablespoons ginger julienne.

2 Heat oil in a medium-sized heavy-based pot and sauté onion, ginger, garlic and salt for 1 minute. Add wine or sherry and simmer for a further minute or until liquid has reduced by half. Stir in corn and stock and bring to the boil. Reduce heat and simmer gently for 30 minutes. During the cooking time you may need to skim the surface of the soup occasionally to remove any impurities.

3 Stir through chicken and soy sauce and simmer for a further minute. Lower heat and slowly pour beaten egg into soup in a thin stream, stirring constantly with a fork. Remove soup from the stove as soon as you see the egg forming fine 'ribbons'.

4 Serve soup in bowls and garnish with spring onions.

Simple Fish Soup

Serve as a starter for 4

There is nothing more health-giving and tantalising than lightly poached fish. Because the fish fillets are sliced into thin pieces, the cooking time is minimal. In Chinese cooking, fish is always 'barely' cooked so as to retain the 'essence' of the fish – its succulence, sweetness and delicacy. The addition of bean sprouts, coriander and mushrooms creates a texture-filled eating experience. Fish that work well in this soup include bar cod, blue eye, flathead, snapper, perch, bream, ling, cod, turbot, halibut and sea bass.

1 bunch bok choy
6 cups Chinese Fish Stock (page 24)
1 tablespoon ginger julienne
1 tablespoon light soy sauce
1 teaspoon white sugar
400 g (13 oz) firm white-fleshed fish fillets,
    cut on the diagonal into 1 cm (½ in) slices

75 g (2½ oz) fresh oyster mushrooms,
    stems discarded and caps halved
1 teaspoon sesame oil
1½ cups fresh bean sprouts
¼ cup coriander (cilantro) sprigs
2 tablespoons finely sliced spring onions
    (scallions)

Remove core from bok choy, cut crossways into 4, then wash thoroughly and drain.

Bring stock to the boil in a large heavy-based pot. Add ginger, soy sauce and sugar and stir to combine. Reduce heat, add fish and simmer gently for 1 minute. Add mushrooms and simmer for 30 seconds. Toss in bok choy and simmer for a further minute or until fish is just cooked through. Stir in sesame oil and remove pot from stove.

Serve in bowls, garnished with bean sprouts, coriander and spring onions.

Simple Vegetable Soup

Serve as a meal for 4

A vegetarian's delight, this soup is loaded with more than ten different vegetables, all varying in colour, size, flavour and texture. One of the most important things in Chinese cooking is creating contrast and balance in every dish. The mint and coriander tossed in at the end give the soup a 'lift'.

1 bunch bok choy
1 small carrot, peeled
1 small cucumber
6 cups Chinese Vegetable Stock (page 27)
1 tablespoon ginger julienne
1 tablespoon light soy sauce
1 teaspoon white sugar
1 small tomato, cut into wedges
75 g (2½ oz) fresh oyster mushrooms, stems discarded and caps halved

90 g (3 oz) snow peas (mange-tout), trimmed and finely sliced
45 g (1½ oz) fresh black cloud ear fungus, roughly chopped
1 cup finely shredded Chinese cabbage
1 teaspoon sesame oil
¼ cup coriander (cilantro) leaves
¼ cup mint leaves
1 large red chilli, finely sliced on the diagonal

Remove core from bok choy, cut crossways into 4, then wash thoroughly and drain.

Using a vegetable peeler, finely slice carrot and cucumber lengthways into ribbons. Cut slices into a fine julienne and set aside.

Bring stock to the boil in a large heavy-based pot. Add ginger, soy sauce and sugar and stir to combine. Reduce heat, add tomato and oyster mushrooms and simmer for 2 minutes. Add bok choy, carrot, snow peas, black cloud ear fungus and cabbage and simmer for a further minute or until vegetables are just tender. Stir in sesame oil and remove pot from stove.

Ladle soup into bowls. Place reserved cucumber, coriander, mint and chilli on a plate and serve alongside soup.

Simple Chicken Soup

Serve as a meal for 4

This dish is an example of taking very simple ingredients and transforming them into something extraordinary. When you use the best-quality homemade stock, seasoned lightly with ginger and soy, to gently poach some chicken – the result is wonderful. There are no tricks to good cooking; to me, it is just about being mindful and caring in all aspects . . . poaching as opposed to boiling, free-range or organic chicken as opposed to hormone- and antibiotic-laden, intensively reared chicken, fresh vegetables as opposed to bruised, old ones.

1 bunch bok choy

6 cups Rich Chinese Chicken Stock (page 22)

2 tablespoons light soy sauce

1 tablespoon ginger julienne

1 teaspoon white sugar

400 g (13 oz) free-range chicken breasts,
    cut on the diagonal into 2 cm (1 in) slices

75 g (2½ oz) fresh shiitake mushrooms,
    stems discarded and caps finely sliced

1 teaspoon sesame oil

1 cup fresh bean sprouts

¼ cup coriander (cilantro) sprigs

¼ cup mint leaves

Remove cores from bok choy, cut crossways into 4, then wash thoroughly and drain.

Bring stock to the boil in a large heavy-based pot. Add soy sauce, ginger and sugar and stir to combine. Reduce heat, add chicken and simmer gently for 1 minute. Add mushrooms and simmer for 2 minutes. Toss in bok choy and simmer for a further minute or until chicken is just cooked through. Stir in sesame oil and remove pot from stove.

Serve soup in bowls, garnished with sprouts, coriander sprigs and mint.

Chicken Noodle Soup

Serve as a meal for 4

When using vacuum-packed, pre-cooked noodles, I tend to rinse the noodles under hot running water prior to adding them to the soup. This aids in untangling them and also rinses away any excess starch. But if you can find fresh Hokkien noodles instead, I would strongly recommend them. They are made from fresh eggs, so treat them as you would fresh pasta (store in the fridge and use within 3 days), then blanch them in a pot of boiling salted water and drain before adding to your soup.

Chicken noodle soup is one of those homey, comfort dishes that people love – and it is very easy to make if you have some stock in your freezer.

½ bunch bok choy

1 × 450 g (15 oz) packet fresh Hokkien noodles

6 cups Rich Chinese Chicken Stock (page 22)

2 tablespoons light soy sauce

1 tablespoon ginger julienne

2 teaspoons oyster sauce

1 teaspoon white sugar

400 g (13 oz) free-range chicken breasts, cut widthways into 1 cm (½ in) slices

1 teaspoon sesame oil

½ cup spring onion (scallion) julienne

2 large red chillies, finely sliced on the diagonal

Remove cores from bok choy, cut crossways into 4, then wash thoroughly and drain.

Place noodles in a colander and rinse well under hot running water, then drain.

Bring stock to the boil in a large heavy-based pot. Add soy sauce, ginger, oyster sauce and sugar and stir to combine. Reduce heat, add drained noodles and simmer gently for 30 seconds. Add bok choy and chicken and simmer for a further 2 minutes or until chicken is just cooked through. Stir in sesame oil, then remove pot from stove.

Ladle soup into large bowls. Place spring onion and chilli in a separate bowl and serve alongside soup.

Seafood Noodle Soup

Serve as a meal for 4

Once you have prepared all the seafood, this dish is really rewarding to put together. If you don't have time to clean whole squid, just ask your fishmonger for ready-cleaned squid hoods. You will notice that the seafood is added at different times to allow for the variation in cooking times – the result is a beautiful, fresh, vibrant soup filled with goodness and a myriad of flavours and textures. Suggested fish types for this soup include blue eye, snapper, bream, ling, cod, halibut and sea bass. The noodles provide a slippery, slurpy backdrop to this hearty meal in a bowl!

250 g (8 oz) small whole squid

16 uncooked medium-sized prawns (shrimp) – about 550 g (1 lb 2 oz)

1 × 450 g (15 oz) packet fresh Hokkien noodles

1 bunch bok choy

6 cups Chinese Fish Stock (page 24)

1 tablespoon light soy sauce

1 tablespoon ginger julienne

1 teaspoon white sugar

200 g (6½ oz) firm white-fleshed fish fillets, cut on the diagonal into 1 cm (½ in) slices

60 g (2 oz) fresh shiitake mushrooms, stems discarded and caps finely sliced

2 teaspoons sesame oil

1 cup fresh bean sprouts

½ cup spring onion (scallion) julienne

¼ cup coriander (cilantro) sprigs

First clean and score the squid (see pages 136–7). Cut scored squid into 1.5 cm (¾ in) strips and set aside.

Peel, de-vein and butterfly prawns (see pages 124–5), leaving tails intact.

Place noodles in a colander and rinse well under hot running water, then drain.

Remove cores from bok choy, cut crossways into 4, then wash thoroughly and drain.

Bring stock to the boil in a large heavy-based pot. Add soy sauce, ginger and sugar and stir to combine. Reduce heat, add prawns and fish and simmer gently for 1 minute. Add reserved squid, drained noodles and mushrooms and simmer for 1 minute. Toss in bok choy and cook for a further minute or until fish is just cooked through. Stir in sesame oil and remove pot from stove.

Serve in bowls and garnish with bean sprouts, spring onion and coriander.

Vegetable Noodle Soup

Serve as a meal for 4

When I think of this soup I think of 'lightness' and 'delicacy' – this is why the vegetables are sliced finely and julienned. I think it is very important to match the preparation technique of an ingredient to the main character of a dish. For me, finely sliced vegetables equate with refinement, making this soup balanced not only in terms of flavour, but also in its overall composition.

1 small cucumber
1 medium-sized carrot, peeled
1 × 220 g (7 oz) packet fresh Hokkien noodles
6 cups Chinese Vegetable Stock (page 27)
¼ cup light soy sauce
1 tablespoon ginger julienne
1 teaspoon white sugar
2 sticks of celery, finely sliced on the diagonal
100 g (3½ oz) fresh oyster mushrooms, stems discarded and caps sliced

150 g (5 oz) fresh shiitake mushrooms, stems discarded and caps sliced
150 g (5 oz) snow peas (mange-tout), trimmed and finely sliced
2⅓ cups finely shredded Chinese cabbage
1 cup fresh bean sprouts
⅓ cup mint leaves
2 large red chillies, finely sliced on the diagonal

Using a vegetable peeler, finely slice cucumber and carrot lengthways into ribbons. Cut slices into a fine julienne and set aside.

Place noodles in a colander and rinse well under hot running water, then drain.

Bring stock to the boil in a large heavy-based pot. Add soy sauce, ginger and sugar and stir to combine. Reduce heat, add drained noodles and celery and simmer for 1 minute. Toss in reserved carrots, mushrooms, snow peas and cabbage and simmer for a further minute or until noodles are just tender. Remove pot from stove.

Ladle soup into bowls. Place reserved cucumber, bean sprouts, mint and chilli in separate bowls and serve alongside soup.

Prawn Wonton Soup

Serve as a starter for 4

There are so many versions of this soup that I think nearly everyone must have tried it at least once in their life. This recipe is beautiful because it is based on the freshest ingredients: the stock is vibrant and aromatic, the prawns are marinated first before being rolled into the wontons, and there is no MSG, which too often finds its way into wonton soups. The flavour is pure and clean and the texture of the boiled wontons is slippery, silky and delectable – comfort food! The addition of fresh Chinese greens creates a complementary texture for the wontons.

½ **bunch choy sum or bok choy**
6 **cups Light Chinese Chicken Stock (page 21)**
1 **tablespoon ginger julienne**
1½ **tablespoons light soy sauce**
1 **teaspoon white sugar**
½ **teaspoon sesame oil**
¼ **cup finely sliced spring onions (scallions)**

Wontons
9 **uncooked medium-sized prawns (shrimp)**
  – about 300 g (10 oz)
1 **tablespoon roughly chopped coriander**
  (cilantro) leaves
1 **tablespoon finely sliced spring onions**
  (scallions)
1½ **teaspoons finely diced ginger**
1 **teaspoon shao hsing wine or dry sherry**
1 **teaspoon light soy sauce**
1 **teaspoon oyster sauce**
¼ **teaspoon white sugar**
¼ **teaspoon sesame oil**
16 **fresh wonton wrappers,**
  about 7 cm (3 in) square

For the wontons, peel and de-vein prawns, then dice prawn meat (see pages 124–5) – you should have about 150 g (5 oz) diced prawn meat. Combine prawn meat and remaining ingredients, except wonton wrappers, in a bowl, cover and refrigerate for 30 minutes.

Next, fill and shape the wontons (see pages 266–7).

Trim 5 cm (2 in) from ends of choy sum and cut crossways into 7 pieces. If using bok choy, remove core and cut crossways into 4. Wash greens thoroughly and drain.

Bring stock to the boil in a large heavy-based pot. Add ginger, soy sauce, sugar and sesame oil and stir to combine. Reduce heat, drop wontons into stock and simmer gently for 2 minutes. Add choy sum or bok choy and simmer for a further minute or until greens and wontons are tender. To test the wontons you will need to remove one using a slotted spoon and cut through it with a sharp knife to see if the prawns are just cooked through.

To serve, divide wontons between bowls, pour in soup and garnish with spring onions.

Hot and Sour Soup

Serve as a meal for 4

You will need about 300 g (10 oz) fresh peas in their pods for this recipe, or you can use frozen peas if fresh ones are out of season.

1 small cucumber
1 × 300 g (10 oz) packet silken tofu
6 cups Light Chinese Chicken Stock (page 21)
2 tablespoons ginger julienne
3 teaspoons sea salt
2 teaspoons white sugar
⅔ cup fresh peas, shelled
1 medium-sized tomato, diced

50 g (1½ oz) fresh shiitake mushrooms, stems discarded and caps sliced
2 tablespoons light soy sauce
1 tablespoon malt vinegar
¼ teaspoon chilli oil
50 g (1½ oz) fresh black cloud ear fungus
3 free-range eggs, lightly beaten
1 cup spring onion (scallion) julienne

Using a vegetable peeler, finely slice cucumber lengthways and then cut into thin slices crossways.

Gently remove tofu from packet and invert on a plate. Carefully cut into 30 cubes (cut lengthways into 5 equal slices, then widthways into 6) and set aside.

Bring stock to the boil in a large heavy-based pot. Add ginger, salt and sugar and stir to combine. Reduce heat, stir in peas and simmer for 1½ minutes. Add reserved tofu, tomato, mushrooms, soy sauce, vinegar and chilli oil and simmer for a further 3 minutes or until peas are just tender.

Toss in black cloud ear fungus and cucumber and simmer for 30 seconds. Lastly, pour beaten egg into soup in a thin stream and immediately remove pot from stove. Stir egg through soup with a fork to form fine 'ribbons'.

Serve in bowls, garnished with spring onion.

beef

Stir-Fried Beef with Oyster Sauce

Serve as a meal for 4 with steamed rice or as part of a banquet for 4–6

600 g (1 lb 4 oz) beef fillet

⅓ cup shao hsing wine
   or dry sherry

1 teaspoon sea salt

1 medium-sized onion

6 slices ginger

3 garlic cloves

⅓ cup vegetable oil

1 tablespoon oyster sauce

1 tablespoon white sugar

1 tablespoon light soy sauce

1 tablespoon malt vinegar

¼ teaspoon sesame oil

3 spring onions (scallions),
   trimmed and cut into
   10 cm (4 in) lengths

2 tablespoons water

pinch ground white pepper

Always use high-quality beef fillet for any stir-fries: the short cooking time and high heat tend to intensify the flavour of the meat, so only the best will do. Beef and oyster sauce make a wonderful pair, as the richness of the oyster sauce is able to stand up to the richness of the beef. I have added some vinegar and sugar to the seasoning – the desired flavour is a balance of salty, sweet and vinegary.

1 Cut beef into 1 cm (½ in) slices. Combine beef with half the wine and salt in a large bowl, cover, and leave to marinate in the refrigerator for 30 minutes. Meanwhile, slice onion and ginger and roughly chop garlic.

2 Heat half the oil in a hot wok until surface seems to shimmer slightly. Add half the marinated beef and stir-fry for 30 seconds. Remove from wok with a slotted spoon and set aside. Add remaining beef and stir-fry for 30 seconds then remove from wok and set aside.

3 Add remaining oil to the hot wok. Stir in onions, ginger and garlic and stir-fry for 1 minute or until onions are lightly browned, stirring constantly to ensure garlic does not burn. Return beef to the wok with remaining wine, oyster sauce, sugar, soy sauce, vinegar and sesame oil and stir-fry for 30 seconds. Lastly, toss in spring onions and water and stir-fry for a further minute or until beef is just tender.

4 Arrange beef on a platter, sprinkle with pepper and serve immediately.

Stir-Fried Beef with Sichuan Pepper and Salt and Lemon

Serve as a meal for 4 with steamed rice or as part of a banquet for 4–6

The secret to this dish is the extended period of marinating. If possible, leave the beef to marinate in the refrigerator overnight, to allow it to become tenderised and absorb the flavours. Make sure the wok is piping hot: basically you are just searing the meat, at the same time caramelising the kecap manis and sugar in the marinade. Finish with the piquant spiciness of Sichuan pepper and salt, balanced with some fresh sour and acidic lemon wedges.

600 g (1 lb 4 oz) beef fillet,
    cut into 1 cm (½ in) slices
2 tablespoons vegetable oil
1 tablespoon shao hsing wine or dry sherry
1 tablespoon white sugar
1 tablespoon light soy sauce
½ teaspoon sesame oil
2 tablespoons Sichuan pepper and salt
    (see page 14)
2 lemons, cut into wedges

Marinade
2 tablespoons shao hsing wine
    or dry sherry
2 tablespoons kecap manis
2 tablespoons white sugar
2 tablespoons roughly diced ginger
3 garlic cloves, finely diced
1 tablespoon oyster sauce
1 tablespoon light soy sauce
2 teaspoons malt vinegar
½ teaspoon sesame oil

Combine beef with marinade ingredients in a large bowl, cover, and leave to marinate in the refrigerator for 2 hours or overnight.

Heat oil in a hot wok until surface seems to shimmer slightly. Add half the marinated beef and stir-fry for 30 seconds. Remove from wok with a slotted spoon and set aside. Add remaining beef and stir-fry for 30 seconds before returning reserved beef to the wok with wine or sherry, sugar, soy sauce and sesame oil. Stir-fry for a further minute or until beef is just tender.

Arrange beef on a platter with a small bowl of Sichuan pepper and salt. Serve immediately with lemon wedges.

Stir-Fried Beef with Black Bean and Chilli Sauce

Serve as a meal for 4 with steamed rice or as part of a banquet for 4–6

A classic Cantonese dish, with a versatile sauce that suits many meats, fish, seafood and tofu.
I like this recipe because it is very colourful and vibrant. Add more chilli if you like it extra hot!

600 g (1 lb 4 oz) beef fillet,
    cut into 1 cm (½ in) slices
⅓ cup vegetable oil
¼ cup finely sliced spring onions (scallions)

Marinade
2 tablespoons shao hsing wine
    or dry sherry
1 teaspoon sea salt
1 teaspoon white sugar

Black Bean and Chilli Sauce
½ medium-sized red pepper
1 small red onion, finely sliced
¼ cup ginger julienne
3 garlic cloves, roughly chopped
1 tablespoon salted black beans
2 tablespoons shao hsing wine
    or dry sherry
1 tablespoon white sugar
1 tablespoon light soy sauce
2 tablespoons oyster sauce
1 tablespoon malt vinegar
½ teaspoon sesame oil
2 large red chillies,
    sliced on the diagonal

Combine beef with marinade ingredients in a large bowl, cover, and leave to marinate in the refrigerator for 30 minutes.

Heat half the oil in a hot wok until surface seems to shimmer slightly. Add half the marinated beef and stir-fry for 30 seconds. Remove from wok with a slotted spoon and set aside. Add remaining beef and stir-fry for 30 seconds then remove from wok and set aside.

Meanwhile, make the Black Bean and Chilli Sauce. Remove seeds and membranes from pepper, cut into fine slices and set aside. Add remaining oil to hot wok. Add onion, ginger, garlic and black beans and stir-fry over a high heat for 30 seconds, stirring constantly to ensure the black beans do not burn.

Return beef to the wok with wine or sherry and stir-fry for 30 seconds. Add sugar, soy sauce, oyster sauce, vinegar and sesame oil and stir-fry for a further minute. Lastly, add chilli and reserved pepper and stir-fry for a further 30 seconds.

To serve, arrange beef on a platter and garnish with spring onions.

Mongolian Beef

Serve as a meal for 4 with steamed rice or as part of a banquet for 4–6

There is something rather yummy about eating things that are finely sliced and shredded, especially with chopsticks. I have always liked picking at tasty morsels, and this dish is perfect for this. I prefer to use beef mince in my Mongolian beef, rather than the usual beef strips, to give it a lighter texture. The slight 'salting' of the Chinese cabbage adds character and complexity. Serve with a bowl of steaming hot rice and some sliced chillies on the side.

600 g (1 lb 4 oz) quality beef mince (ground beef)
5 cups finely shredded Chinese cabbage
2 teaspoons sea salt
¼ cup vegetable oil
2 tablespoons shao hsing wine or dry sherry
2 tablespoons hoisin sauce
1 tablespoon oyster sauce
1 teaspoon malt vinegar
½ teaspoon sesame oil
1 small carrot, peeled and finely sliced
½ medium-sized red pepper, finely sliced
¾ cup finely sliced spring onions (scallions)

Marinade
2 tablespoons shao hsing wine or dry sherry
1 tablespoon light soy sauce
1 tablespoon cornflour (cornstarch)
1 tablespoon finely diced ginger
3 garlic cloves, finely diced
½ teaspoon sesame oil

Combine beef mince with marinade ingredients in a large bowl, cover, and leave to marinate in the refrigerator for 30 minutes.

Meanwhile, place cabbage and salt in a large bowl, mixing together well with your hands to combine. Stand for 15 minutes then rinse under cold water and drain. Use your hands to squeeze out any excess liquid.

Heat 2 tablespoons of the oil in a hot wok until surface seems to shimmer slightly. Add half the marinated beef and stir-fry for 30 seconds, breaking up any lumps with a wok spoon. Remove from the wok with a slotted spoon and set aside.

Add remaining oil to hot wok, stir in remaining beef and cook, stirring for 30 seconds. Return reserved beef mixture to the wok with wine or sherry, hoisin sauce, oyster sauce, vinegar and sesame oil and stir-fry for 30 seconds.

Toss in reserved cabbage, carrot and pepper and stir-fry for a further minute. Stir through spring onions, reserving just a little to garnish, and remove from heat.

Spoon beef into a serving bowl, sprinkle with remaining spring onions and serve.

Dry-Fried Sichuan Beef

2 × 300 g (10 oz) beef fillets

1½ cups vegetable oil

1 tablespoon vegetable oil, extra

2 large red chillies, finely sliced

1 tablespoon finely diced ginger

3 garlic cloves, finely diced

2 tablespoons hoisin sauce

2 teaspoons Sichuan pepper
and salt (see page 14)

1 cup finely sliced spring onions
(scallions)

pinch Sichuan pepper and salt,
extra

½ cup finely shredded iceberg
lettuce leaves

Serve as a meal for 4 with steamed rice or as part of a banquet for 4–6

Sichuan cuisine is one of my favourites – I love hot food. For this dish, the beef fillets are semi-frozen before cutting, which allows you to slice them into super-fine strips. The finished dish is filled with interesting textures; it has no 'sauce' but is deliciously crunchy, salty and spicy all at once.

1 Wrap beef fillets in plastic cling wrap. Place on a tray in the freezer for about 30 minutes or until slightly firm, so they are easy to slice finely without tearing. Remove plastic cling wrap and, using a sharp knife, cut beef fillets into 5 mm (¼ in) slices, then cut slices into 5 mm (¼ in) strips.

2 Heat oil in a hot wok until surface seems to shimmer slightly. Add half the beef and stir-fry for 1 minute, stirring constantly to prevent beef sticking together. Remove from wok with a slotted spoon, drain well on kitchen paper and set aside. Repeat process with remaining beef. Remove excess oil from wok and wipe clean.

3 Heat extra oil in the same hot wok. Stir in chilli, ginger and garlic and cook on medium heat for 30 seconds, stirring constantly to ensure garlic does not burn. Return beef to the wok with hoisin sauce and stir-fry for a further 30 seconds. Add Sichuan pepper and salt and stir-fry for 30 seconds. Lastly, stir through spring onions.

4 Arrange beef on a platter, sprinkle with extra Sichuan pepper and salt, and top with lettuce.

pork

Sung Choi Bao of Pork

Serve as a starter for 4

1 small carrot, peeled

4 small iceberg lettuce leaves

2 tablespoons peanut oil

1 tablespoon ginger julienne

1 garlic clove, finely diced

200 g (6½ oz) pork mince
(ground pork)

½ small red onion, finely sliced

2 fresh shiitake mushrooms, stems
discarded and caps sliced

2 tablespoons shao hsing wine
or dry sherry

1 tablespoon light soy sauce

1 teaspoon white sugar

1 teaspoon oyster sauce

¼ teaspoon sesame oil

1 stick of celery, finely diced

½ cup fresh bean sprouts

¼ cup finely sliced spring onions
(scallions)

handful coriander (cilantro) sprigs

Texture! Texture! Texture! All the ingredients for this sung choi bau are finely sliced and cooked at different times throughout the stir-fry – this allows each individual ingredient to 'sing'. The result is a delicious, tasty meat mixture which is then wrapped up in a cold, crunchy iceberg lettuce leaf and devoured! This is a favourite at Billy Kwong – people just love the fun of eating with their fingers. Some Chinese restaurants serve very ordinary versions of this dish that consist of little more than stir-fried beef or pork mince with a splash of hoisin. The result is one dimensional, uninspiring and completely lacking in texture. To ensure the success of this dish, fatty pork mince is essential; the higher the fat content of the pork, the more moist and tender the final result will be.

1 Using a vegetable peeler, finely slice carrot lengthways into ribbons. Cut carrot into a fine julienne and set aside.

2 Soak lettuce leaves in cold water for 1 hour, drain them well and set aside, covered, in the refrigerator.

3 Heat peanut oil in a hot wok and stir-fry ginger, garlic and pork mince for 1 minute. Add onions and mushrooms and continue stir-frying for 20 seconds.

4 Pour in wine or sherry, soy sauce, sugar, oyster sauce and sesame oil and stir-fry for 1 minute or until pork is cooked through. Toss in reserved carrot, celery, bean sprouts and spring onions and stir to combine.

5 Remove pork mixture from wok using a slotted spoon to ensure you leave any juices in the wok. Serve in a bowl set on a large platter, garnished with coriander and accompanied with lettuce-leaf cups. To eat, simply spoon pork mixture into lettuce cups, roll up to enclose the filling and eat with your fingers!

Stir-Fried Pork Fillets with Honey and Ginger

Serve as a meal for 4 with steamed rice or as part of a banquet for 4–6

If possible, marinate the pork overnight for better flavour!

600 g (1 lb 4 oz) pork fillets,
    cut into 5 mm (¼ in) slices
¼ cup vegetable oil
2 spring onions (scallions), trimmed
    and cut into 10 cm (4 in) lengths
1 tablespoon malt vinegar
1 tablespoon light soy sauce
1 tablespoon water
2 limes, halved

Marinade
2 tablespoons honey
2 tablespoons light soy sauce
2 tablespoons shao hsing wine or dry sherry
2 tablespoons finely diced ginger
1 tablespoon oyster sauce
2 teaspoons dark soy sauce
2 teaspoons five-spice powder
½ teaspoon sesame oil

Combine pork with marinade ingredients in a large bowl, cover, and leave to marinate in the refrigerator for 30 minutes or overnight.

Heat 2 tablespoons of the oil in a hot wok until surface seems to shimmer slightly. Add half the marinated pork and stir-fry for 30 seconds. Remove from wok with a slotted spoon and set aside. Heat remaining oil in the wok, add remaining pork and stir-fry for another 30 seconds. Return reserved pork to the wok with spring onions, vinegar, soy sauce and water. Stir-fry for a further minute or until pork is just cooked through and lightly browned.

Arrange pork on a platter and serve with lime halves.

Stir-Fried Pork Fillets with Hoisin Sauce

Serve as a meal for 4 with steamed rice or as part of a banquet for 4–6

Chinese people just love their pork! It is cooked in many different ways – when stir-frying it is important to slice the fillets finely so cooking time is quick and flavour is vibrant. Because pork is quite rich, I have used an intense sauce, hoisin, in this recipe.

600 g (1 lb 4 oz) pork fillets,
    cut into 5 mm (¼ in) slices
1 small cucumber
2 tablespoons vegetable oil
1 tablespoon light soy sauce

Marinade
3 garlic cloves, finely diced
¼ cup hoisin sauce
2 tablespoons malt vinegar
2 tablespoons shao hsing wine
    or dry sherry
1 tablespoon light soy sauce
2 teaspoons white sugar
1 teaspoon five-spice powder
½ teaspoon sesame oil
½ teaspoon sea salt

Combine pork with marinade ingredients in a large bowl, cover, and leave to marinate in the refrigerator for 30 minutes.

Using a vegetable peeler, finely slice cucumber lengthways into ribbons. Set aside.

Heat oil in a hot wok until surface seems to shimmer slightly. Add half the marinated pork and stir-fry for 30 seconds. Remove from wok with a slotted spoon and set aside. Add remaining pork with all the marinade and stir-fry for 30 seconds. Return reserved pork to the wok with soy sauce and stir-fry for a further minute or until pork is just cooked through and lightly browned.

Serve immediately, garnished with reserved cucumber.

Sweet and Sour Pork

Serve as a meal for 4 with steamed rice or as part of a banquet for 4–6

1½ tablespoons cornflour
    (cornstarch)
1 tablespoon cold water
2 × 300 g (10 oz) pork neck fillets,
    cut in half lengthways and
    then into bite-sized pieces
    on the diagonal
2 egg yolks, lightly beaten
3 teaspoons light soy sauce
2 teaspoons sesame oil
1 teaspoon sea salt
¼ cup plain (all-purpose) flour
¼ cup cornflour (cornstarch), extra
vegetable oil for deep-frying

Sweet and Sour Sauce
¼ small ripe pineapple, peeled
1 small carrot, peeled
1 small cucumber, peeled
¾ cup malt vinegar
5 tablespoons shao hsing wine
    or dry sherry
½ cup white sugar
1 teaspoon sea salt, extra
4 garlic cloves, crushed
2 tablespoons ginger julienne
½ medium-sized yellow pepper,
    julienned
2 small tomatoes, finely sliced
2 tablespoons light soy sauce

I find that marinating the pork overnight is a must for this dish – the flavour is so much more intense. I guess the main difference between my sweet and sour sauce and traditional recipes is that I use fresh tomatoes instead of tomato sauce out of the bottle, fresh pineapple instead of tinned pineapple.

1 Blend cornflour with water in a medium-sized bowl until dissolved. Add pork, egg yolks, soy sauce, sesame oil and salt and mix well. Cover and leave to marinate in the refrigerator overnight.

2 To make the Sweet and Sour Sauce, remove core from pineapple and finely slice into pieces. Using a vegetable peeler, finely slice carrot lengthways into ribbons. Cut cucumber in half lengthways, slice on the diagonal and set aside, together with the pineapple and carrot.

3 Place vinegar, wine or sherry, sugar and extra salt in a medium-sized heavy-based saucepan and stir over high heat until sugar dissolves. Bring to the boil, add garlic and ginger, reduce heat and simmer, uncovered, for 10 minutes. Add reserved pineapple, carrot, cucumber, pepper and tomato and simmer for a further 3 minutes or until pineapple is tender and tomato has broken down slightly. Stir in soy sauce, remove from stove and set aside.

4 Combine plain flour and extra cornflour. Add to the marinated pork and mix well. Heat vegetable oil in a hot wok until surface seems to shimmer slightly. Deep-fry pork in batches over high heat for 1 minute, then reduce heat to medium and fry for another 2 minutes, or until pork is almost cooked through. Remove from wok and drain on kitchen paper. Gently reheat Sweet and Sour Sauce. Finally, return all pork to the hot wok and deep-fry for a further 3 minutes, or until lightly browned, crispy and cooked through. Remove from wok and drain well on kitchen paper.

5 Arrange pork on a platter and serve immediately with a bowl of warm Sweet and Sour Sauce.

chicken

White-Cooked Chicken
with Soy and Ginger Dressing

Serve as part of a banquet for 4–6

1 × 1.6 kg (3 lb 4 oz) free-range
    chicken
2 tablespoons peanut oil
¼ cup coriander (cilantro) sprigs
pinch ground white pepper

White Master Stock

6 litres (6 quarts) cold water
3 cups shao hsing wine or dry sherry
8 spring onions (scallions), trimmed
    and cut in half crossways
12 garlic cloves, crushed
1½ cups ginger slices
⅓ cup sea salt

Soy and Ginger Dressing

¼ cup light soy sauce
2 tablespoons White Master Stock
1 teaspoon sesame oil
½ teaspoon white sugar
⅓ cup spring onion (scallion)
    julienne
1 tablespoon ginger julienne

I could eat this dish four times a week – the texture is so silky and I love the savoury flavours. The poaching and steeping technique used in this recipe is perfect for cooking chicken, as it is very gentle; the integrity of the chicken is preserved, and the result is moist, tender flesh. The heating of the peanut oil is vital to release its beautiful, nutty flavour and bring out the aroma of the soy and ginger. Always use the best-quality chicken – you might pay slightly more, but you'll appreciate the difference, and the accompanying ingredients cost little. Pages 76–7 show how to chop up a chicken 'Chinese-style' – we Chinese just love chomping on those bones!

1 Place all stock ingredients in a large stockpot and bring to the boil. Reduce heat and simmer gently for 40 minutes to allow the flavours to infuse.

2 Rinse chicken under cold water. Trim away excess fat from inside and outside cavity, but keep neck, parson's nose and winglets intact. Lower chicken, breast-side down, into simmering stock, ensuring it is fully submerged. Poach chicken gently for exactly 14 minutes. There should be no more than an occasional ripple breaking the surface; adjust the temperature, if necessary, to ensure stock does not reach simmering point again. Remove stockpot immediately from the stove and allow chicken to steep in the stock for 3 hours at room temperature to complete the cooking process. Using tongs, gently remove chicken from the stock, being careful not to tear the breast skin. Place chicken on a tray to drain and allow to cool.

3 Meanwhile, make the dressing: combine soy sauce, stock, sesame oil, sugar, spring onion and ginger in a bowl and set aside. Heat peanut oil in a small frying pan until moderately hot and carefully pour over dressing.

4 Chop the chicken Chinese-style (see pages 76–7), arrange on a platter and pour dressing over chicken. Garnish with coriander and sprinkle with pepper.

CHOPPING A CHICKEN OR DUCK CHINESE-STYLE

Place cooled chicken or duck on chopping board, breast side up.

With a sharp knife or cleaver, make an incision along the centre of the breast.

Using the heel of your hand, apply pressure to the top of your knife to chop through the breast bone.

Make an incision between the drumstick/ thigh and the breast.

Cut bony pieces from the breast and discard.

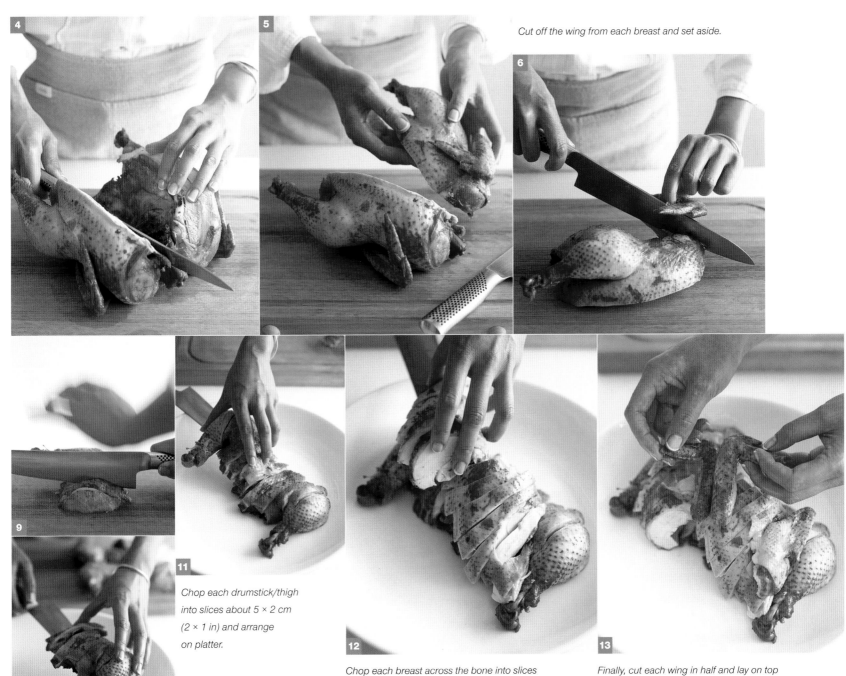

Ease apart the two halves of the chicken or duck with your hands and the knife.

Cut down one side of the backbone to separate the two breasts.

Cut off the wing from each breast and set aside.

Chop each drumstick/thigh into slices about 5 × 2 cm (2 × 1 in) and arrange on platter.

Chop each breast across the bone into slices about 7 × 2 cm (3 × 1 in). Arrange on top of drumstick/thigh pieces as shown.

Finally, cut each wing in half and lay on top of chicken or duck.

Soy Sauce Chicken

Serve as part of a banquet for 4–6

**1 × 1.6 kg (3 lb 4 oz) free-range
chicken**

Red Master Stock

**3 cups shao hsing wine
or dry sherry**

2 cups dark soy sauce

1 cup light soy sauce

2 cups brown sugar

12 garlic cloves, crushed

1 cup ginger slices

**8 spring onions (scallions),
trimmed and cut in half
crossways**

1 teaspoon sesame oil

10 star anise

4 cinnamon quills

7 strips fresh orange zest

The addition of dark soy and light soy to the master stock turns it into Red Master Stock – all those beautiful, reddish-brown chickens you see hanging up in the windows of Chinese barbecue shops are poached in this stock, which is often called Red Braise Stock. Because the chicken has been steeped for 3 hours, it has an amazing intensity of colour from the soy and flavour from the aromatics – subtle hints of ginger, star anise, cinnamon and orange zest. This stock can be reused again and again by simply straining it thoroughly, storing it in an airtight container and freezing it. Each time you use this stock, it will become richer and deeper: simply thaw it and add a fresh batch of all the stock ingredients, plus enough water to make up the volume of liquid to 6 litres (6 quarts) again.

1 Place all stock ingredients, plus 6 litres (6 quarts) of cold water, in a large stockpot and bring to the boil. Reduce heat and simmer gently for 40 minutes to allow the flavours to infuse. Meanwhile, rinse chicken under cold water. Trim away excess fat from inside and outside cavity, but keep neck, parson's nose and winglets intact.

2 Lower chicken, breast-side down, into simmering stock, ensuring it is fully submerged. Poach chicken gently for exactly 14 minutes. There should be no more than an occasional ripple breaking the surface; adjust the temperature, if necessary, to ensure stock does not reach simmering point again. Remove stockpot immediately from the stove and allow chicken to steep in the stock for 3 hours at room temperature to complete the cooking process.

4 Chop the chicken Chinese-style (see pages 76–7) and arrange on a platter. Spoon over some of the master stock and serve at room temperature.

3 Using tongs, gently remove chicken from the stock, being careful not to tear the breast skin. Place chicken on a tray to drain and allow to cool.

Stir-Fried Chicken Fillets with Cashews

Serve as a meal for 4 with steamed rice or as part of a banquet for 4–6

This is perhaps one of the most frequently ordered dishes in Chinese restaurants. I particularly like the addition of cold, refreshing cucumber right at the last moment.

800 g (1 lb 10 oz) chicken thigh fillets,
    cut into 2 cm (1 in) slices
1 medium-sized cucumber
¼ cup vegetable oil
1 cup unsalted and roasted cashew nuts –
    about 150 g (5 oz)
6 garlic cloves, finely diced
2 tablespoons shao hsing wine or dry sherry
2 teaspoons sea salt
¾ cup finely sliced spring onions (scallions)

Marinade
2 tablespoons shao hsing wine
    or dry sherry
2 tablespoons cornflour (cornstarch)
1 tablespoon cold water
1 teaspoon sea salt

Combine chicken with marinade ingredients in a large bowl, cover, and leave to marinate in the refrigerator for 30 minutes.

Cut cucumber in half lengthways and scoop out the seeds using a spoon. Place cucumber cut-side down on a chopping board, finely slice on the diagonal and set aside.

Heat 2 tablespoons of the oil in a hot wok until surface seems to shimmer slightly. Add half the marinated chicken and stir-fry for 1 minute. Remove from wok with a slotted spoon and set aside. Add remaining chicken and stir-fry for 1 minute, remove from wok and set aside.

Add remaining oil to the hot wok, stir in nuts and garlic and stir-fry on medium heat for 30 seconds, stirring constantly to ensure garlic does not burn. Immediately return chicken to the wok and increase heat to high. Pour in wine or sherry and stir-fry for 30 seconds. Add salt and continue to stir-fry for a further 30 seconds or until chicken is lightly browned and just cooked through. Lastly, add reserved cucumber and stir-fry for 10 seconds.

Arrange chicken on a platter, garnish with spring onions and serve immediately.

Stir-Fried Chicken Fillets with Honey and Ginger

Serve as a meal for 4 with steamed rice or as part of a banquet for 4–6

Marinating the chicken overnight gives this dish a rich, luscious flavour – the honey caramelises when stir-fried and the addition of five-spice powder gives this dish that unmistakable Chinese aroma.

**800 g (1 lb 10 oz) chicken thigh fillets,
  cut into 2 cm (1 in) slices**
2 tablespoons vegetable oil
1 tablespoon light soy sauce

Marinade
¼ cup honey
2 tablespoons light soy sauce
**2 tablespoons shao hsing wine
  or dry sherry**
2 tablespoons finely diced ginger
1 tablespoon oyster sauce
2 teaspoons dark soy sauce
2 teaspoons five-spice powder
½ teaspoon sesame oil

Combine chicken with marinade ingredients in a large bowl, cover, and leave to marinate in the refrigerator overnight.

Heat oil in a hot wok until surface seems to shimmer slightly. Add half the marinated chicken with the marinade and stir-fry for 1 minute. Remove from wok with a slotted spoon and set aside. Add remaining chicken and stir-fry for 1 minute. Return reserved chicken to the wok with soy sauce and stir-fry for a further 2 minutes or until chicken is just cooked through and slightly caramelised.

Arrange chicken on a platter and serve.

Stir-Fried Chicken Fillets
with Asparagus and Baby Corn

Serve as a meal for 4 with steamed rice or as part of a banquet for 4–6

I particularly love the texture of asparagus and baby corn when stir-fried. They are sweet and crunchy and also the colours are beautiful and vibrant. A luscious, rich coating is created on the chicken by adding a dash of cornflour to the marinade.

It is only necessary to peel the asparagus if they are large.

800 g (1 lb 10 oz) chicken thigh fillets,
   cut into 2 cm (1 in) slices
1 bunch green asparagus – about 250 g (8 oz)
¼ cup vegetable oil
125 g (4 oz) fresh baby corn, cut in half
   lengthways
3 spring onions (scallions), trimmed
   and cut into 10 cm (4 in) lengths
6 cm (2½ in) knob ginger, finely sliced
2 tablespoons shao hsing wine or dry sherry
2 tablespoons water
1 tablespoon light soy sauce
2 teaspoons white sugar
¼ teaspoon sesame oil
¼ cup finely sliced spring onions
   (scallions)

Marinade
2 tablespoons shao hsing wine
   or dry sherry
2 tablespoons cornflour (cornstarch)
1 tablespoon cold water
1 teaspoon sea salt

Combine chicken with marinade ingredients in a large bowl, cover, and leave to marinate in the refrigerator for 30 minutes.

Wash asparagus and trim woody ends. Peel lower parts of the stems, if necessary, and finely slice on the diagonal. Set aside.

Heat 2 tablespoons of the oil in a hot wok until surface seems to shimmer slightly. Add half the marinated chicken and stir-fry for 1 minute. Remove from wok with a slotted spoon and set aside. Add remaining chicken and stir-fry for 1 minute, remove from wok and set aside.

Add remaining oil to the hot wok, stir in corn, spring onions and ginger and stir-fry for 30 seconds. Add reserved asparagus and stir-fry for a further 30 seconds. Return chicken to the wok, add wine or sherry and stir-fry for 30 seconds. Lastly, add water, soy sauce, sugar and sesame oil and stir-fry for a further minute or until chicken is lightly browned and just cooked through.

Arrange chicken on a platter and top with finely sliced spring onions.

Lemon Chicken Fillets

Serve as a meal for 4 with steamed rice or as part of a banquet for 4–6

2 tablespoons cornflour
   (cornstarch)
2 tablespoons cold water
800 g (1 lb 10 oz) chicken
   thigh fillets, cut into
   2 cm (1 in) slices
2 egg yolks
2 tablespoons shao hsing wine
   or dry sherry
1 teaspoon sea salt
2 cups Light Chinese Chicken
   Stock (page 21)
⅓ cup shao hsing wine
   or dry sherry, extra
2 tablespoons oyster sauce
¼ cup hoisin sauce
1 tablespoon light soy sauce
1 tablespoon white sugar
1 teaspoon sea salt, extra
7 strips fresh lemon zest
1 small lemon, finely sliced
⅓ cup plain (all-purpose) flour
⅓ cup cornflour (cornstarch), extra
vegetable oil for deep-frying
2 tablespoons lemon juice
¼ cup coriander (cilantro) sprigs

There are so many versions of this Cantonese classic – this is mine. The lemon sauce is at once rich, salty, sour and sweet; the addition of hoisin adds a mysterious, spicy note; and the acidity of the lemon balances the overall flavour.

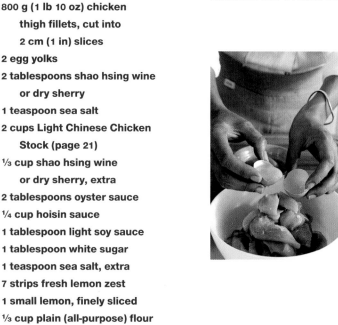

1 Blend cornflour with water in a medium-sized bowl until dissolved. Add chicken, egg yolks, wine or sherry and salt to cornflour mixture and mix well. Cover and leave to marinate in the refrigerator for 1 hour.

2 Place stock, extra wine or sherry, oyster sauce, hoisin sauce, soy sauce, sugar, extra salt and lemon zest in a medium-sized saucepan and bring to the boil. Reduce heat and simmer gently, uncovered, for about 10 minutes or until slightly reduced and the flavours are balanced. Stir in sliced lemon and simmer for a further 5 minutes — do not cook any longer or the sauce will turn bitter. Remove from heat and set aside.

3 Combine plain flour and extra cornflour, add to the marinated chicken and mix well. Heat oil in a hot wok until surface seems to shimmer slightly. Deep-fry half the chicken over high heat for 1 minute, then reduce heat to medium and fry for a further minute, or until chicken is almost cooked through.

4 Remove from wok and drain on kitchen paper. Repeat process with remaining chicken. Finally, return all the chicken to the hot oil and deep-fry for a further minute or until lightly browned, crispy and just cooked through. Be careful not to overcook the chicken at this stage or it may become too dry. Remove from the wok and drain well on kitchen paper.

5 Gently reheat lemon sauce, stir in lemon juice and remove from heat. Arrange chicken on a platter, garnish with coriander, and serve immediately with a bowl of hot lemon sauce.

Soy Sauce Chicken Wings with Fresh Shiitake Mushrooms

Serve as a meal for 4 with steamed rice or as part of a banquet for 4–6

A beautiful way to cook chicken is to poach and then steep it in this Red Master Stock. This gentle cooking method creates the silkiest chicken wings ever and a great sauce is created simply by reducing some of the poaching liquid with sugar and fresh shiitake mushrooms.

12 large chicken wings – about 1.5 kg (3 lb)
4 fresh shiitake mushrooms, stems discarded and caps sliced
2 tablespoons brown sugar
¼ cup spring onion (scallion) julienne

Red Master Stock

6 litres (6 quarts) cold water
3 cups shao hsing wine or dry sherry
2 cups dark soy sauce
1 cup light soy sauce
2 cups brown sugar
12 garlic cloves, crushed
1 cup ginger slices
8 spring onions (scallions), trimmed and cut in half crossways
1 teaspoon sesame oil
10 star anise
4 cinnamon quills
7 strips fresh orange zest

Place all stock ingredients in a large stockpot and bring to the boil. Reduce heat and simmer gently for 40 minutes to allow the flavours to infuse.

Lower chicken wings into simmering stock. Cover with a cartouche (see page 6) to ensure they are fully submerged, and simmer gently for exactly 7 minutes. There should be no more than an occasional ripple breaking the surface; adjust the temperature, if necessary, to ensure stock does not reach simmering point again.

Remove stockpot immediately from the stove and allow wings to steep in the stock for 15 minutes at room temperature to complete the cooking process.

Meanwhile, place 2 cups of master stock in a medium-sized saucepan and bring to the boil. Reduce heat, stir in mushrooms and sugar, and simmer for about 3 minutes or until mushrooms are tender.

Using a large slotted spoon, gently remove wings from stock, being careful not to tear the skin. Arrange chicken wings on a platter and spoon over reduced master stock and mushrooms. Sprinkle with spring onions and serve.

Deep-Fried Chicken Wings with Chilli, Salt and Lemon

Serve as a starter for 4–6

This recipe is dead simple and absolutely delicious. By steaming the chicken wings first, you are basically cooking them through – the deep-frying is for texture, and the chilli salt coating is perfectly complemented by a squeeze of sour lemon! You could steam the chicken wings several hours before deep-frying and just place them in the fridge. Make sure the chicken wings are drained thoroughly before rolling in chilli-salt – this will ensure a crispier finish when deep-fried.

12 large chicken wings – about 1.5 kg (3 lb)
⅓ cup plain (all-purpose) flour
1½ tablespoons chilli powder
1½ tablespoons sea salt
vegetable oil for deep-frying

4 large red chillies, cut in half lengthways
**   and seeds removed**
¼ cup spring onion (scallion) julienne
2 lemons, halved

Arrange chicken wings on a heatproof plate that will fit inside a steamer basket. Place plate inside steamer and position over a deep saucepan or wok of boiling water and steam, covered, for 4 minutes.

Carefully remove plate from steamer basket, drain away excess liquid and set aside for 15 minutes to cool slightly.

Meanwhile, combine flour, chilli powder and salt in a large bowl. Add chicken wings in two batches and toss to coat well, shaking off any excess flour.

Heat oil in a hot wok until surface seems to shimmer slightly. Add half the wings and deep-fry for about 7 minutes or until just cooked through and lightly browned. Using tongs, turn wings occasionally to ensure even cooking. Remove with a slotted spoon and drain well on kitchen paper. Repeat process with remaining wings.

Add chillies to the same hot oil and fry for about 1 minute or until they are a deep bright red. Remove with a slotted spoon and drain well.

Arrange chicken wings on a platter and garnish with fried chillies and spring onions. Serve immediately with lemon halves.

duck

Chilli-Salt Duck Breasts with Lemon

Serve as a meal for 4 with steamed rice or as part of a banquet for 4–6

4 × 200 g (6½ oz) duck breasts,
    with skin, trimmed of excess fat

2 tablespoons plain (all-purpose)
    flour

3 teaspoons chilli powder

3 teaspoons sea salt

vegetable oil for deep-frying

2 tablespoons Sichuan pepper
    and salt (see page 14)

1 large red chilli, finely sliced
    on the diagonal

2 tablespoons spring onion
    (scallion) julienne

2 lemons, halved

This is one of my favourite dishes in this book. It is so simple yet so tasty and impressive – impressive because many people are wary of handling duck. If you feel intimidated about preparing duck (it really is not that difficult), then please try this recipe using duck breasts. You steam the breasts then roll them in chilli-salt for flavour, and deep-fry for texture. Serve with Sichuan pepper and salt and fresh lemon. YUM!

1 Arrange duck breasts, skin-side up, on a heatproof plate that will fit inside a steamer basket. Place plate inside steamer, position over a deep saucepan or wok of boiling water and steam, covered, for 12 minutes or until duck breasts are half cooked.

2 Meanwhile, in a large bowl, combine flour, chilli powder and salt. Carefully remove plate from steamer basket, transfer duck breasts to a rack and set aside for 25 minutes to cool slightly.

3 Add duck breasts to chilli-salt mixture and toss to coat well, shaking off any excess flour. Heat oil in a large hot wok until surface seems to shimmer slightly. Add duck breasts and deep-fry for about 2 minutes or until just cooked through and lightly browned then remove and drain well on kitchen paper.

4 Cut duck on the diagonal into 1 cm (½ in) slices and arrange on a platter with a small bowl of Sichuan pepper and salt. Garnish with chilli and spring onion and serve immediately with lemon halves.

Mum's Stir-Fried Duck Breasts with Carrot, Onion and Celery

Serve as a meal for 4 with steamed rice or as part of a banquet for 4–6

This dish always reminds me of my mother's wonderful, simple home cooking. The combination of carrot, onion and celery is seen a lot in Cantonese cooking, with both meat and seafood dishes.

4 × 200 g (6½ oz) duck breasts, with skin
2 small carrots, peeled
1 tablespoon vegetable oil
1 small white onion, cut in half and
   then into wedges
1 stick of celery, sliced on the diagonal
⅓ cup water
1 tablespoon malt vinegar

Marinade
2 tablespoons shao hsing wine or dry sherry
2 tablespoons light soy sauce
1 tablespoon white sugar
2 teaspoons oyster sauce
1 teaspoon sesame oil
1 teaspoon finely grated fresh ginger

Trim excess fat from duck breasts – you should have about 600 g (1lb 4 oz) duck after trimming – and cut on the diagonal into 1 cm (½ in) slices.

Combine duck with marinade ingredients in a large bowl, cover, and leave to marinate in the refrigerator for 30 minutes.

Cut carrots in half lengthways, finely slice on the diagonal and set aside.

Heat 1 teaspoon of the oil in a hot wok, add half the marinated duck and stir-fry for 1 minute. Remove from wok with a slotted spoon and set aside. Add remaining duck and stir-fry for 1 minute, then remove from wok and set aside.

Remove excess oil from the wok and wipe clean. Heat remaining oil in the same hot wok, add reserved carrot, onion and celery and stir-fry for 1 minute. Return duck to the wok and stir-fry for 30 seconds. Pour in water, reduce heat to medium and simmer, uncovered, for 1 minute. Lastly, add vinegar and simmer for a further minute or until duck is just tender.

Arrange duck on a platter and serve.

Stir-Fried Duck Breasts with Honey and Ginger

Serve as a meal for 4 with steamed rice or as part of a banquet for 4–6

If possible, marinate the duck overnight for a rich, luscious flavour!

4 × 200 g (6½ oz) duck breasts, with skin
1 teaspoon vegetable oil
¼ cup water
juice of 2 limes

Marinade
¼ cup honey
2 tablespoons light soy sauce
2 tablespoons shao hsing wine or dry sherry
2 tablespoons finely diced fresh ginger
1 tablespoon oyster sauce
2 teaspoons dark soy sauce
1½ teaspoons five-spice powder
½ teaspoon sesame oil

Trim excess fat from duck breasts – you should have about 600 g (1 lb 4 oz) duck after trimming – and cut on the diagonal into 1 cm (½ in) slices.

Combine duck with marinade ingredients in a large bowl, cover, and leave to marinate in the refrigerator for 30 minutes or overnight.

Heat oil in a hot wok, add half the marinated duck and stir-fry for 1 minute. Remove from wok with a slotted spoon and set aside. Add remaining duck with all the marinade juices and stir-fry for 1 minute. Finally, return reserved duck to the wok with water, reduce heat to medium and simmer, uncovered, for 2 minutes or until duck is just tender.

Arrange duck on a platter and serve with lime juice in a separate bowl.

seafood

4 ×

⅓ c
2 ta

2 ta
1 Ch
½ te
2 ta
¼ te
½ c

1½
¼ c
pinc

Deep-Fried Whole Fish with Spring Onion, Ginger and Vinegar Dressing

Serve as part of a banquet for 4–6

The texture of a whole deep-fried fish is amazing! It makes for interesting eating, and we Chinese just love chewing and sucking on all the bones and weird bits. Because the fish is deep-fried, I team it with a rather pungent dressing – the vinegar, kecap manis (which tastes like sweet, thick soy sauce) and chilli oil create the most deliciously sweet, salty, sour, spicy combination. I like to sit the whole fish on a bed of iceberg lettuce to create extra texture and respite from the strong flavours. Suggested fish types for this recipe are ocean perch, snapper, sand whiting, pigfish, John Dory, sea bass, halibut, sole and flounder.

1 × 750 g (1 lb 8 oz) whole fish, scaled, cleaned and gutted
vegetable oil for deep-frying
2 iceberg lettuce leaves
2 tablespoons finely sliced spring onions (scallions)
pinch Sichuan pepper and salt (see page 14)

Spring Onion, Ginger and Vinegar Dressing
2½ tablespoons light soy sauce
2 tablespoons finely sliced coriander (cilantro) roots and stems
2 tablespoons finely diced ginger
2 tablespoons finely sliced spring onions (scallions)
2 tablespoons kecap manis
2 tablespoons malt vinegar
¼ teaspoon chilli oil
dash of sesame oil

Combine all dressing ingredients in a bowl and set aside.

Pat fish dry with kitchen paper and place on a chopping board. With a sharp knife, make four diagonal slits into one side of the fish, then score in the opposite direction to make a diamond pattern. Turn fish and repeat on the other side.

Heat vegetable oil in a hot wok until surface seems to shimmer slightly. Carefully lower fish into the wok so it is completely covered by the oil, fry for 3 minutes, then carefully turn fish and fry for a further 3 minutes or until fish is lightly browned and just cooked through when tested. The flesh should be white through to the bone; if it is still translucent, cook for another minute or so.

Arrange lettuce leaves on a large serving plate. Using a spatula, carefully remove fish from wok and drain on kitchen paper. Transfer to the serving plate, pour over reserved dressing and garnish with spring onions. Sprinkle with Sichuan pepper and salt and serve immediately.

Soy Sauce Fish Fillets

Serve as a meal for 4 with steamed rice or as part of a banquet for 4–6

Here is another use of the classic Red Master Stock, with hints of aniseed, cinnamon, soy, ginger, garlic and orange. Lightly poached in this wonderfully intense and interesting stock, fillets of fish gain depth and complexity of flavour. Suggested fish for this recipe include salmon, ocean trout, blue eye, Murray cod, red emperor, mahi mahi, barramundi, halibut or sea bass.

4 × 100 g (3½ oz) fish fillets
1 bok choy, core removed

Red Master Stock
6 cups cold water
¾ cup shao hsing wine or dry sherry
½ cup dark soy sauce
¼ cup light soy sauce
½ cup brown sugar
3 garlic cloves, crushed
¼ cup ginger slices
**2 spring onions (scallions), trimmed
    and cut in half crossways**
¼ teaspoon sesame oil
2 star anise
1 cinnamon quill
2 strips fresh orange zest

Place all stock ingredients in a wide deep pan – about 30 cm (12 in) wide × 5 cm (2 in) deep – and bring to the boil. Reduce heat and simmer gently for 40 minutes to allow flavours to infuse.

Lower fish into simmering stock and cover with a cartouche (see page 6) to ensure it is fully submerged. Poach fish gently for exactly 2 minutes; there should be no more than an occasional ripple breaking the surface. Immediately remove pan from the stove and allow fish to steep in the stock for 5 minutes to complete the cooking process.

Meanwhile, separate bok choy leaves and wash thoroughly. Add bok choy to a saucepan of boiling salted water and blanch for 30 seconds or until almost tender. Drain immediately.

Using a slotted spoon, gently remove fish from stock and transfer to a serving bowl. Spoon ⅔ cup of the master stock, along with some whole spices and aromatics, over fish. Top with bok choy and serve immediately.

Deep-Fried Whole Fish
with Sichuan Pepper and Salt

Serve as part of a banquet for 4–6

I love the simplicity of this dish – minimal ingredients, maximum flavour. Buy the freshest fish available and be sure to use clean oil for deep-frying. Suitable fish for this recipe are snapper, bream, King George whiting, silver perch, ocean perch, pigfish, sand whiting, barramundi, cod, halibut and sea bass. The classic combination of Sichuan pepper and salt teamed with fresh lemon is seen time and time again in Chinese cuisine.

1 × 750 g (1 lb 8 oz) whole fish, scaled, cleaned and gutted
¾ cup plain (all-purpose) flour
vegetable oil for deep-frying
2 large red chillies

handful coriander (cilantro) sprigs
¼ cup spring onion (scallion) julienne
2 lemons, halved
1 tablespoon Sichuan pepper and salt (see page 14)

Pat fish dry with kitchen paper and place on a chopping board. With a sharp knife, make four diagonal slits into one side of the fish, then score in the opposite direction to make a diamond pattern. Turn fish and repeat on the other side. Lightly toss fish in flour to coat.

Meanwhile, heat oil in a hot wok until surface seems to shimmer slightly. Carefully lower fish into the wok so it is completely covered by the oil, fry for 3 minutes, then carefully turn fish and fry for a further 3 minutes or until fish is lightly browned and just cooked through when tested. The flesh should be white through to the bone; if it is still translucent, cook for another minute or so. Using a spatula, carefully remove fish from wok and drain on kitchen paper.

Add chillies to same hot oil and fry until they are a deep bright red colour. Remove with a slotted spoon and drain well.

Transfer fish to a large platter and garnish with combined coriander, spring onion and fried chillies. Serve immediately with lemon halves and Sichuan pepper and salt.

King Prawn Toasts

Serve as a starter for 4 (makes about 12 prawn toasts)

16 uncooked king prawns (jumbo shrimp) – about 800 g (1 lb 10 oz)

¼ cup spring onion (scallion) julienne

¼ cup finely chopped coriander (cilantro) leaves

1 tablespoon ginger julienne

2 teaspoons shao hsing wine or dry sherry

1 teaspoon light soy sauce

1 egg white, lightly beaten

½ teaspoon sea salt

6 slices thick white bread

¼ cup sesame seeds

vegetable oil for deep-frying

Sweet Chilli and Carrot Dipping Sauce

½ small carrot, peeled

½ teaspoon white sugar

½ teaspoon sea salt

2 cups rice wine vinegar

1½ cups white sugar, extra

5 tablespoons fish sauce

2 large red chillies, finely sliced on the diagonal

This recipe is so cool! What is wacky about this dish is that you think to yourself, 'How does the prawn mixture stay on the bread slices once it is lowered into the hot oil?' Well, all I can say is follow the recipe, roll the toasts in sesame seeds on both sides, and see for yourself – it is like MAGIC!!!

As children we always felt it was a bit of a treat when Mum served King Prawn Toasts, as they were usually reserved for special occasions only. They are definitely a crowd pleaser, and most impressive. I like to serve them with a pungent, sweet and spicy dipping sauce.

1 To make the sauce, finely slice carrots lengthways into ribbons using a vegetable peeler. Cut ribbons into a fine julienne. Combine carrots in a bowl with sugar and salt, mix well and leave to stand for 10 minutes. Drain carrots and using your hands, gently squeeze away any excess liquid.

2 Meanwhile, place vinegar and extra sugar in a medium-sized heavy-based saucepan and bring to the boil. Reduce heat and simmer, uncovered, for about 15 minutes or until reduced by almost half and slightly syrupy. Remove from stove, ladle into bowl of pickled carrots, fish sauce and chilli and set aside.

3 Peel and de-vein prawns, then cut prawn meat into 1.5 cm (¾ in) dice (see pages 124–5).

4 In a bowl, combine prawn meat with remaining ingredients except bread, sesame seeds and vegetable oil, and mix well.

5 Remove and discard crusts from bread and cut each slice in half. Place a tablespoon of prawn mixture onto each piece of bread, lightly pressing mixture onto bread to cover well. Gently roll each piece of prawn bread in sesame seeds to lightly coat.

6 Heat oil in a hot wok until surface seems to shimmer slightly. Working in batches, carefully lower prawn toasts, prawn-side down, into hot oil. Deep-fry on medium heat for 1 minute. Turn toasts over and cook other side for a further minute, or until lightly browned all over and just cooked through. Remove from wok using a slotted spoon and drain on kitchen paper.

7 Serve immediately with a bowl of Sweet Chilli and Carrot Dipping Sauce.

Steamed King Prawns with Ginger and Spring Onions

Serve as part of a banquet for 4–6

This is a wonderful example of the dictum that when using the freshest ingredients, you do not have to do too much to them. Buy the best-quality king prawns available, simply steam for 5 minutes or so, then dress them with ginger and shallots and scald with hot peanut oil – and the result is an elegant and delicious dish.

16 uncooked king prawns (jumbo shrimp) – about 800 g (1 lb 10 oz)
⅔ cup water
⅓ cup shao hsing wine or dry sherry
2 tablespoons ginger julienne
⅔ cup finely sliced spring onions (scallions)

1 teaspoon white sugar
2 tablespoons light soy sauce
¼ teaspoon sesame oil
2 tablespoons peanut oil
pinch ground white pepper

Peel, de-vein and butterfly prawns (see pages 124–5), leaving tails intact.

In a shallow heatproof bowl that will fit inside a steamer basket, arrange prawns side-by-side and cover with water and wine or sherry. Top with ginger then place bowl inside steamer and position over deep saucepan or wok of boiling water and steam, covered, for about 5 minutes or until prawns are just cooked through.

Carefully remove bowl from steamer, transfer prawns to a serving bowl and pour over juices. Sprinkle with spring onions, sugar, soy sauce and sesame oil.

Heat peanut oil in a small frying pan until moderately hot, then carefully pour over prawns. Sprinkle with pepper and serve immediately.

eggs

Soy Sauce Eggs

Serve as part of a banquet for 4

A very simple interpretation of the classic Chinese 'thousand year old' eggs. These eggs are great served as an appetiser with Chinese pickles – like a Chinese version of antipasto. I love the deep, mahogany reddish-brown the soy sauce turns the eggs.

6 free-range eggs
1 cup light soy sauce
2 tablespoons dark soy sauce

1 cup water
½ cup brown sugar
10 ginger slices

Place eggs in a small saucepan of boiling water and cook for about 6 minutes. Remove eggs from the saucepan with a slotted spoon and refresh under cold running water. Peel eggs and set aside.

Meanwhile, combine soy sauces, water, sugar and ginger in a small heavy-based saucepan and bring to the boil for 1 minute. Reduce heat, add eggs and simmer, covered with a cartouche (see page 6), for 1 hour, turning occasionally. Remove saucepan from stove and set aside, covered, for 30 minutes, turning eggs occasionally.

Remove eggs from the saucepan, reserving 1 tablespoon of the braising stock for garnish. Discard remaining stock.

To serve, cut each egg in half lengthways and arrange on a platter. Spoon over reserved braising stock.

Soft-Boiled Eggs with Oyster Sauce and Chilli

Serve as a starter for 4 or as part of a banquet for 4–6

This dressing is really yummy – the vinegar cuts through the velvety richness of the oyster sauce and the sesame oil adds depth. Once again, because eggs are naturally rich, they need an intensely flavoured sauce to stand up to them.

6 free-range eggs
1 tablespoon oyster sauce
2 teaspoons malt vinegar
½ teaspoon sesame oil

1 large green chilli, finely sliced
on the diagonal
pinch ground white pepper

Place eggs in a small saucepan of boiling water and cook for about 4 minutes. Remove eggs from saucepan with a slotted spoon and refresh under cold running water.

Meanwhile, in a bowl, combine oyster sauce, vinegar and sesame oil.

Carefully peel eggs, cut in half and arrange on a platter. Spoon over oyster sauce mixture, top with chillies and sprinkle with pepper. Serve immediately.

Soft-Boiled Eggs with Tomato and Chilli Salad

Serve as a starter for 4 or as part of a banquet for 4–6

You could also use hard-boiled eggs for this recipe, if you prefer them. I am addicted to the crunch of iceberg lettuce, especially with eggs – the contrast in textures is amazing – and the tomato adds a refreshing zing.

6 free-range eggs
⅓ cup brown sugar
2 tablespoons water
3 teaspoons light soy sauce
2 teaspoons malt vinegar

¼ small iceberg lettuce
1 medium-sized tomato, cut into wedges
1 large green chilli, finely sliced
   on the diagonal
pinch ground white pepper

Place eggs in a small saucepan of boiling water and cook for about 4 minutes. Remove eggs from saucepan using a slotted spoon and refresh under cold running water.

Meanwhile, combine sugar and water in a small heavy-based saucepan and stir over heat until sugar dissolves. Stir in soy sauce and vinegar and remove from stove.

Tear lettuce leaves into large pieces, arrange on a serving platter and top with tomato wedges. Carefully peel eggs, cut in half and place on top of tomatoes. Spoon over sauce and garnish with chillies. Sprinkle with pepper and serve immediately.

tofu

Tofu and Celery Salad

This is a delightful summer dish – light and fresh, simple and tasty. I blanch the celery
so it is easy to digest and then add a dressing that is a lovely balance of salty, sour and sweet.

1 stick of celery, finely sliced on the diagonal
1 small carrot, peeled
1 × 200 g (6½ oz) packet five-spice pressed tofu,
   finely sliced
1 cup spring onion (scallion) julienne
1 cup fresh bean sprouts
½ cup coriander (cilantro) leaves
1 tablespoon roasted sesame seeds
pinch Sichuan pepper and salt (see page 14)

Dressing
2 tablespoons light soy sauce
2 teaspoons white sugar
2 teaspoons malt vinegar
½ teaspoon sesame oil
3 garlic cloves, finely diced
1 tablespoon peanut oil

Add celery to a small saucepan of boiling salted water and blanch for 30 seconds. Drain, refresh under cold water and drain again.

Using a vegetable peeler, finely slice carrots lengthways into ribbons and set aside.

To make the dressing, combine all ingredients, except peanut oil, in a heatproof bowl. Heat peanut oil in a small frying pan until moderately hot, then carefully pour over dressing ingredients to release the flavours. Stir to combine.

Combine reserved celery and carrots in a large bowl with remaining ingredients, pour over dressing and mix thoroughly using your hands. Serve salad in a bowl.

Steamed Silken Tofu with Ginger and Spring Onions

Serve as part of a banquet for 4–6

Sometimes simple is best – and you just cannot go past the unique and amazingly sensual texture of silken tofu.

1 × 300 g (10 oz) packet silken tofu
1 tablespoon shao hsing wine or dry sherry
⅓ cup water
1 tablespoon light soy sauce
½ teaspoon white sugar
1 tablespoon ginger julienne

¼ cup spring onion (scallion) julienne
1 tablespoon peanut oil
1 teaspoon sesame oil
pinch Sichuan pepper and salt
 (see page 14)

Gently remove tofu from packet and invert into a shallow heatproof bowl that will fit inside a steamer basket. Carefully cut widthways into 8 equal slices. Cover with wine or sherry, water, soy sauce, sugar and half the ginger, then place bowl inside steamer, position over a deep saucepan or wok of boiling water and steam, covered, for about 6 minutes or until heated through. Carefully remove bowl from steamer and using a spatula transfer tofu, with its liquid, to a shallow serving bowl. Top with spring onion and remaining ginger.

Heat peanut oil in a small frying pan until moderately hot, then carefully pour over tofu to release the flavours. Sprinkle with sesame oil and Sichuan pepper and salt before serving immediately.

Stir-Fried Tofu with Vegetables

Serve as part of a banquet for 4–6

I must stress the importance of slicing ingredients finely when stir-frying: not only do they cook correctly, but the overall look is wild – so much movement and colour!

1 small carrot, peeled
1 medium-sized zucchini (courgette)
½ medium-sized red pepper
2 tablespoons peanut oil
1 × 200 g (6½ oz) packet five-spice pressed tofu, finely sliced
1 medium-sized red onion, finely sliced
1 tablespoon ginger julienne

¼ cup shao hsing wine or dry sherry
2 teaspoons white sugar
2 teaspoons light soy sauce
2 teaspoons malt vinegar
1 teaspoon oyster sauce
½ teaspoon sesame oil
1 cup spring onion (scallion) julienne

Cut carrot and zucchini in half lengthways, then finely slice on the diagonal. Remove seeds and membranes from pepper and cut into fine slices.

Heat oil in a hot wok until surface seems to shimmer slightly. Add carrot, tofu, onion and ginger and stir-fry for 1 minute. Add wine or sherry, zucchini, pepper and sugar and stir-fry for 1 minute. Pour in soy sauce, vinegar, oyster sauce and sesame oil and stir-fry for a further minute or until vegetables are just tender. Toss in spring onion, stir-fry for 10 seconds, then remove from heat.

Transfer to a shallow bowl and serve immediately.

Deep-Fried Tofu with Black Bean and Chilli Sauce

Serve as a starter for 4 or as part of a banquet for 4–6

The substantial and robust flavours of black bean and chilli sauce work miracles with tofu simply coated in flour and then deep-fried.

1 × 300 g (10 oz) packet silken tofu
vegetable oil for deep-frying
⅓ cup plain (all-purpose) flour
pinch Sichuan pepper and salt (see page 14)

Black Bean and Chilli Sauce
¼ medium-sized red pepper
1 tablespoon vegetable oil
½ small red onion, finely sliced
1 tablespoon ginger julienne
2 small garlic cloves, roughly chopped
2 teaspoons salted black beans
1 tablespoon shao hsing wine or dry sherry
2 teaspoons light soy sauce
2 teaspoons oyster sauce
2 teaspoons white sugar
2 teaspoons malt vinegar
¼ teaspoon sesame oil
1 large red chilli, sliced on the diagonal
⅓ cup water

To make the Black Bean and Chilli Sauce, remove seeds and membranes from pepper, cut into fine slices and set aside. Add oil to a hot wok, add onion, ginger, garlic and black beans and stir-fry over high heat for 1 minute, stirring constantly to ensure black beans do not burn. Add wine or sherry and stir-fry for 20 seconds then add soy sauce, oyster sauce, sugar, vinegar and sesame oil and stir-fry for 30 seconds. Toss in chilli and reserved pepper and stir-fry for 30 seconds. Lastly pour in water and simmer for a further 30 seconds.

Gently remove tofu from packet and invert onto a plate. Carefully slice into 6 cubes by cutting tofu lengthways in half, then widthways into thirds, draining off any excess liquid.

Heat oil in a hot wok until surface seems to shimmer slightly. Lightly coat tofu pieces in flour, and using a spatula, carefully lower into hot oil – *it is important not to coat the tofu in advance of heating the oil, or it will become very moist and sticky.* Deep-fry tofu for about 4 minutes or until lightly browned and crisp. Remove with a slotted spoon and drain well on kitchen paper.

Arrange tofu in a shallow bowl and spoon over Black Bean and Chilli Sauce. Sprinkle with Sichuan pepper and salt and serve immediately.

Deep-Fried Tofu with Sichuan Pepper and Salt and Lemon

Serve as a starter for 4 or as part of a banquet for 4–6

1 × 300 g (10 oz) packet silken tofu

vegetable oil for deep-frying

⅓ cup plain (all-purpose) flour

handful coriander (cilantro) leaves

1 teaspoon Sichuan pepper and
    salt (see page 14)

1 lemon, halved

How simple is this dish, yet so sophisticated. Good cooking is all about treating ingredients with respect and knowing how to handle them – knowing how to bring out the best in ingredients.

1 Cut around edges of cellophane with a sharp knife then gently remove tofu from packet and invert onto a plate. Carefully slice into 6 cubes by cutting tofu lengthways in half, then widthways into thirds, draining off any excess liquid.

2 Heat oil in a hot wok until surface seems to shimmer slightly. Lightly coat tofu pieces in flour and using a spatula, carefully lower into the hot oil – *it is important not to coat the tofu in advance of heating the oil, or it will become very moist and sticky.*

3 Deep-fry tofu for about 4 minutes or until lightly browned and crisp. Remove with a slotted spoon or 'spider' and drain well on kitchen paper.

4 Arrange tofu on a platter, garnish with coriander and serve immediately, sprinkled with Sichuan pepper and salt and accompanied by lemon halves.

Braised Silken Tofu with Pork and Chilli

Serve as part of a banquet for 4–6

This dish is inspired by a famous Sichuanese dish called Ma Po Tofu ('grandmother's bean curd'), which is interesting for its combination of pork with tofu – a most unusual pairing of ingredients yet one that absolutely works. The cuisine of Sichuan is also famous for its ZING! Authentic versions of this dish are fiery hot – laden with Sichuan chilli oil, chilli flakes and whole dried chillies. I love the silky, velvety texture of tofu; it just drinks up the surrounding flavours of sautéed pork, ginger and garlic, soy and oyster sauces, chilli, and Sichuan pepper and salt. The freshly sliced iceberg and tomato add contrast, interesting texture and relief from the chilli. Definitely a dish for tofu addicts!

1 × 300 g (10 oz) packet silken tofu
2 tablespoons vegetable oil
200 g (6½ oz) pork mince (ground pork)
4 garlic cloves, finely diced
1 tablespoon finely diced ginger
⅓ cup shao hsing wine or dry sherry
1 tablespoon white sugar
1 tablespoon light soy sauce
2 teaspoons oyster sauce
½ teaspoon sesame oil

1 teaspoon ground Sichuan pepper
    and salt (see page 14)
⅓ cup water
2 teaspoons malt vinegar
½ teaspoon chilli oil
1 cup finely shredded iceberg lettuce
1 small tomato, finely sliced
2 tablespoons finely sliced spring onions
    (scallions)
pinch Sichuan pepper and salt, extra

Gently remove tofu from packet and invert onto a plate. Carefully cut into 20 cubes by cutting lengthways into 4 equal slices, then widthways into 5.

Heat oil in a hot wok until surface seems to shimmer slightly. Add pork, garlic and ginger and stir-fry for 1 minute. Add wine or sherry, sugar, soy sauce, oyster sauce, sesame oil and Sichuan pepper and salt and stir-fry for 30 seconds. Pour in water and stir-fry for a further 30 seconds. Carefully slide tofu into wok with vinegar and chilli oil, gently separating tofu as it falls into pork mixture. Reduce heat and simmer, uncovered, for 3 minutes or until pork is cooked through.

Spoon braised tofu into a shallow bowl and top with lettuce and tomato. Garnish with spring onions and sprinkle with extra Sichuan pepper and salt.

vegetables

Stir-Fried Chinese Mustard Greens

Serve as part of a banquet for 4–6

One of the lesser known Chinese vegetables, mustard greens (or 'gai choy') is one of my favourites for its unusual, slightly bitter flavour. You can also purchase a pickled version of mustard greens that is strong, salty and intense – it is delicious finely sliced and then stir-fried.

2 bunches mustard greens (gai choy)
¼ cup peanut oil
2 teaspoons sea salt
5 garlic cloves, crushed

¼ cup Light Chinese Chicken Stock
(page 21) or water
2 teaspoons sesame oil

Trim 5 cm (2 in) from ends of mustard greens, cut bunch crossways into 3 lengths, wash thoroughly, then drain.

Heat peanut oil in a hot wok until surface seems to shimmer slightly. Add salt and garlic and stir-fry for 10 seconds. Add mustard greens and stir-fry for 1½ minutes. Pour in stock and stir-fry for a further 30 seconds or until leaves are tender. Lastly, add sesame oil and serve immediately.

Stir-Fried Carrots, Zucchini and Celery

Serve as part of a banquet for 4–6

Three humble ingredients lightly cooked – healthy, tasty and balanced.

2 medium-sized carrots, peeled

2 medium-sized zucchini (courgettes)

2 tablespoons peanut oil

2 sticks of celery, finely sliced on the diagonal

1 medium-sized red onion, roughly sliced

6 ginger slices

3 garlic cloves, crushed

¼ cup shao hsing wine or dry sherry

2 tablespoons light soy sauce

1 tablespoon malt vinegar

2 teaspoons white sugar

½ teaspoon sesame oil

Cut carrots and zucchini in half lengthways and then into 5 mm (¼ in) slices on the diagonal.

Heat peanut oil in a hot wok until surface seems to shimmer slightly. Add carrots, zucchini, celery, onion, ginger and garlic and stir-fry for 2 minutes. Add wine or sherry and stir-fry for 10 seconds. Lastly, add soy sauce, vinegar, sugar and sesame oil and stir-fry for a further 2 minutes or until vegetables are just tender. Serve immediately.

salads

Soy-Dipped Radish Salad

Serve as a side dish to accompany a meal or as part of a banquet for 4–6

Marinating the radishes in salt and sugar for 30 minutes softens their raw heat and makes this a wonderful, tasty, savoury side dish for a large banquet.

6 red radishes, trimmed and cut into 5 mm (¼ in) slices
2 tablespoons white sugar
2 teaspoons sea salt

Dressing
1 tablespoon light soy sauce
1 tablespoon brown sugar
1 teaspoon sesame oil
¼ teaspoon chilli oil

Place radishes in a bowl and sprinkle with sugar and salt. Combine well using your hands, then set aside for 30 minutes.

Meanwhile, to make the dressing, place soy sauce, sugar, sesame oil and chilli oil in a small bowl and stir to combine.

Drain reserved radishes and, using your hands, gently squeeze away any excess liquid. Place radishes in a serving bowl and drizzle with dressing.

Tofu, Black Cloud Ear Fungus, Asian Herb and Sesame Salad

Serve as a starter for 4 or as part of a banquet for 4–6

1 small carrot, peeled

1 small cucumber, cut in half lengthways

1 teaspoon sea salt

1 cup white vinegar

¼ cup white sugar

75 g (2½ oz) five-spice pressed tofu

⅓ cup fresh black cloud ear fungus

⅓ cup spring onion (scallion) julienne

¼ cup coriander (cilantro) leaves

¼ cup sweet Thai basil leaves

¼ cup mint leaves

½ cup finely shredded Chinese cabbage

2 teaspoons roasted sesame seeds

pinch Sichuan pepper and salt (see page 14)

Dressing

1 tablespoon light soy sauce

½ teaspoon sesame oil

1 tablespoon malt vinegar

¼ teaspoon chilli oil

You will not find this salad in downtown Chinatown, but all the principles behind it come from Chinese cuisine. It is fresh, aromatic and light, yet filled with depth and complexity. By pickling the carrots ever so slightly, we give the salad 'body' that we can then build on by adding soy sauce, chilli oil, sesame and so on. This is another fixture on the Billy Kwong menu. I just love eating this salad, whether it's summer or winter – it is SO GOOD FOR YOU!!!

1 Using a vegetable peeler, finely slice carrot and cucumber lengthways into ribbons. Cut carrot ribbons into a fine julienne then place in a bowl with half the salt and mix well. Place cucumber in a separate bowl with remaining salt and mix well. Set cucumber and carrot aside for 1 hour.

2 Combine vinegar and sugar in a small heavy-based saucepan and stir over heat until sugar dissolves. Simmer, uncovered, and without stirring, for about 10 minutes or until reduced and slightly syrupy. Set aside to cool. Drain cucumber and carrot and, using your hands, gently squeeze away any excess liquid. Place vegetables in the cooled syrup to lightly 'pickle' them.

3 Finely slice five-spice pressed tofu. In a large bowl, combine pickled vegetables with all the remaining ingredients except sesame seeds and Sichuan pepper and salt. Mix thoroughly using your hands.

4 To make the dressing, combine ingredients in a small bowl. Spoon dressing over salad. Serve salad on a platter, sprinkled with sesame seeds and Sichuan pepper and salt.

Chilled Cucumber Salad

Serve as a side dish to accompany a meal or as part of a banquet for 4–6

This is yummy on a hot summer's day! When you peel cucumber and sprinkle it with sugar and salt, then chill it, it takes on whole different tone – slippery, silky, yet still crunchy – and the ginger and garlic add a rustic element.

5 small cucumbers, peeled
1 tablespoon white sugar
1 teaspoon sea salt
pinch ground black pepper

Dressing
2 tablespoons light soy sauce
2 garlic cloves, finely diced
1 tablespoon finely diced ginger
½ teaspoon sesame oil

Cut cucumber in half lengthways and scoop out the seeds using a spoon. Place cut-side down on a chopping board and cut on the diagonal into 1.5 cm (¾ in) pieces. Place cucumber in a bowl, sprinkle with sugar and salt and mix well. Cover and refrigerate for 30 minutes.

Meanwhile, to make the dressing, place all ingredients in a small bowl and stir to combine.

Drain cucumbers and, using your hands, gently squeeze away any excess liquid. Combine chilled cucumber in a serving bowl with dressing, sprinkle with pepper and serve immediately.

Prawn and Mint Salad

Serve as a main meal for 4 or as part of a banquet for 4–6

This dish is all about simplicity and freshness! Lightly poach the prawns, throw in finely sliced vegetables and mint then combine with a fresh, vibrant, balanced, smooth dressing for a perfect light summer meal.

**16 cooked medium-sized prawns
(shrimp) – about 550 g (1 lb 2 oz)**
1 small carrot, peeled
1 medium-sized cucumber, peeled
2 cups finely shredded iceberg lettuce
1 stick of celery, finely sliced on the diagonal
⅔ cup spring onion (scallion) julienne
¼ cup roughly torn mint leaves

Dressing
¼ cup quality extra virgin olive oil
2 tablespoons malt vinegar
2 tablespoons light soy sauce
2 teaspoons white sugar

Peel and de-vein prawns (see pages 124–5) and set aside.

Using a vegetable peeler, finely slice carrot lengthways into ribbons. Cut cucumber in half lengthways and scoop out the seeds using a spoon. Place cut-side down on a chopping board and finely slice on the diagonal.

To make the dressing, place all ingredients in a small bowl and stir to combine.

In a separate bowl, combine prawns, carrot and cucumber with remaining ingredients. Pour over dressing and toss well.

Arrange salad on a platter and serve immediately.

rice

Mum's Fried Rice

Serve as a meal for 4 or as part of a banquet for 4–6

4 free-range eggs

⅓ cup vegetable oil

1 small white onion, finely diced

1 tablespoon finely diced ginger

2 rindless bacon rashers,
    finely diced

2 teaspoons white sugar

2 tablespoons shao hsing wine
    or dry sherry

4 cups Steamed Rice (page 249)

⅔ cup finely sliced spring onions
    (scallions)

2 tablespoons light soy sauce

¼ teaspoon sesame oil

The best thing about Mum's Fried Rice is that most people's fridges contain some eggs, bacon and onions, so this incredibly tasty and satisfying meal is a great standby. It's also simple to make – thanks, Mum!!!

1 Break eggs into a bowl and beat lightly. Heat half the oil in a hot wok until surface seems to shimmer slightly. Pour beaten eggs into wok and leave to cook on the base of the wok for 10 seconds before folding egg mixture over onto itself with a spatula and lightly scrambling for about 1 minute or until almost cooked through. Carefully remove omelette from wok with a spatula and drain on kitchen paper. Set aside.

2 Heat remaining oil in hot wok and stir-fry onion, ginger and bacon for 1 minute. Add sugar and stir-fry for 30 seconds. Pour in wine or sherry and stir-fry for 1 minute.

3 Add rice to wok with spring onions, soy sauce, sesame oil and reserved omelette and stir-fry for 2 minutes or until well combined and rice is heated through. Use a spatula to break up the omelette into smaller pieces while cooking. Transfer rice to a bowl and serve.

Egg Fried Rice

Serve as a meal for 4 or as part of a banquet for 4–6

Only use the freshest eggs for this. By scrambling them first, you retain the very best qualities of the eggs – fluffy, light texture and vibrant yellow hue. This is delicious served with some freshly sliced chillies.

6 free-range eggs
⅔ cup finely sliced spring onions (scallions)
2 tablespoons light soy sauce
1 tablespoon finely diced ginger
2 tablespoons vegetable oil

1 small red onion, finely diced
4 cups Steamed Rice (page 249)
1 tablespoon light soy sauce, extra
1⅓ cups finely shredded Chinese cabbage leaves

Place eggs in a bowl with spring onions, soy sauce and ginger and beat lightly with a fork to combine.

Heat oil in a hot wok until surface seems to shimmer slightly. Add onion and stir-fry for 30 seconds. Pour in egg mixture and leave to cook for 10 seconds before folding egg mixture over onto itself with a spatula and lightly scrambling for about 1½ minutes or until almost cooked through. Add rice and extra soy sauce and stir-fry for about 1½ minutes, using a spatula to break up the egg into smaller pieces. Lastly, toss in cabbage and stir-fry for 20 seconds or until well combined and rice is heated through.

Transfer rice to a bowl and serve.

noodles and
wontons

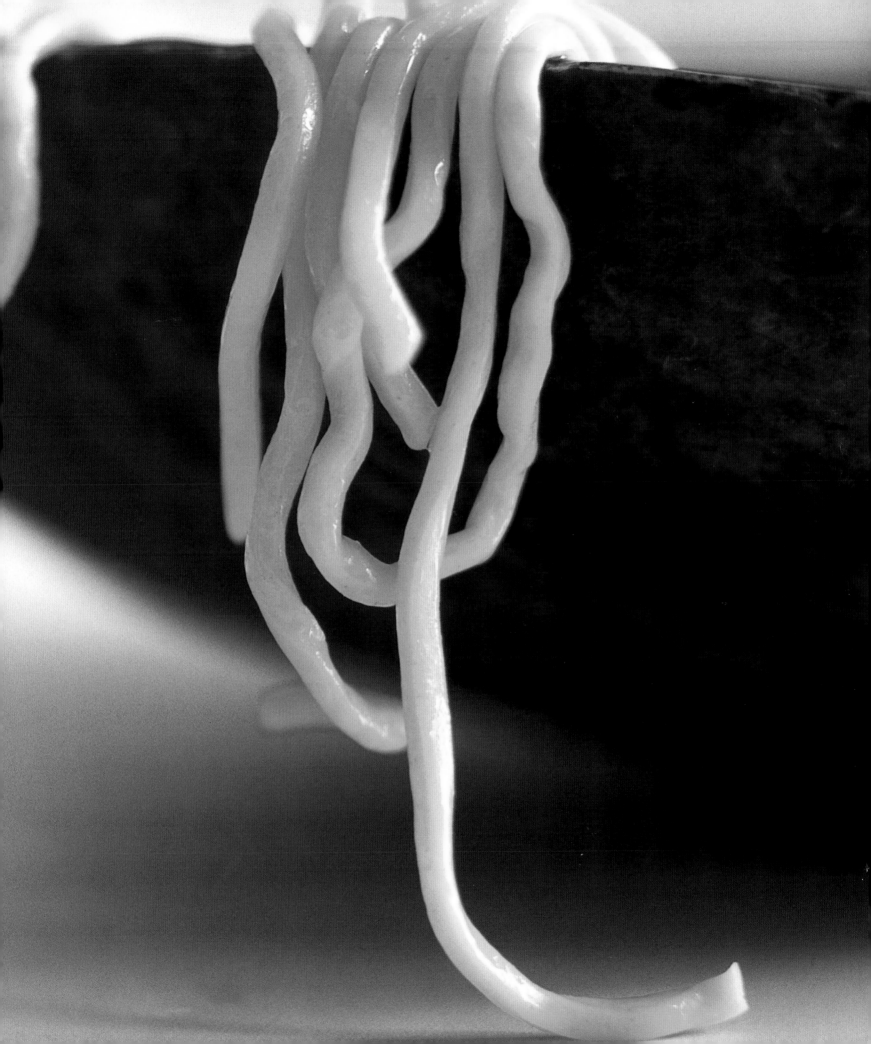

Prawn Wontons with Spring Onion, Ginger and Vinegar Dressing

Serve as a starter for 4

When wontons are boiled, not deep-fried, the result is like little soft pillows. The dressing is inspired by sauces made in the Sichuan province of China – it has a wonderful balance of sweet, sour, salty and spicy, and the coriander, spring onion and ginger fill the sauce with lots of chewy, yummy bits!

2½ tablespoons light soy sauce
2 tablespoons finely sliced coriander
**   (cilantro) roots and stems**
2 tablespoons finely diced ginger
2 tablespoons finely sliced spring onions
**   (scallions)**
2 tablespoons kecap manis
2 tablespoons malt vinegar
¼ teaspoon chilli oil
dash of sesame oil

Wontons
9 uncooked medium-sized prawns
**   (shrimp) – about 300 g (10 oz)**
1 tablespoon roughly chopped coriander
**   (cilantro) leaves**
1 tablespoon finely sliced spring onions
**   (scallions)**
1½ teaspoons finely diced ginger
1 teaspoon shao hsing wine or dry sherry
1 teaspoon light soy sauce
1 teaspoon oyster sauce
¼ teaspoon white sugar
¼ teaspoon sesame oil
16 fresh wonton wrappers,
**   about 7 cm (3 in) square**

Combine soy sauce, coriander, ginger, spring onions, kecap manis, vinegar and both oils in a bowl and set aside.

For the wontons, peel and de-vein prawns, then dice prawn meat (see pages 124–5) – you should have about 150 g (5 oz) diced prawn meat. Combine prawn meat with remaining ingredients, except wonton wrappers, in a bowl, cover and refrigerate for 30 minutes.

Next, fill and shape the wontons (see pages 266–7).

Bring a large saucepan of water to the boil. Drop wontons, in batches, into the water and cook for 2 minutes or until they are just cooked. To test the wontons you will need to remove one using a slotted spoon and cut into it with a sharp knife to see if the prawns are cooked through. Remove wontons with a slotted spoon and drain. Repeat process with remaining wontons.

Arrange wontons on a platter and serve immediately, drizzled with dressing.

FILLING AND SHAPING WONTONS

Dip your finger in water and moisten the bottom edge of the wrapper.

Place a rounded teaspoon of the filling in the centre of a wonton wrapper.

Hold the wonton lengthways between your hands with the folded edge facing down.

Fold the wrapper in half, towards you,
to enclose the filling

Press lightly to seal.

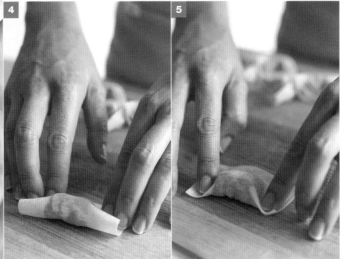

Finally, taking the two ends in your fingers, bring
them together with a twisting action, and press
lightly to join.

Repeat with remaining filling
and wrappers.

Fold the sealed edge of the wonton back on
itself then lightly moisten one corner of the
folded edge with water.

Crispy Prawn Wontons with Sweet Chilli Sauce

Serve as a starter for 4

An absolute classic and all-time favourite Chinese dish! We serve hundreds of these every week at Billy Kwong. I love it when you bite into the crunchy wonton wrapper and then hit a piece of piping hot prawn! These are great as an appetiser or for cocktail food at a party. The chilli sauce is rich, sweet and salty – perfect for deep-fried food.

2 cups rice wine vinegar
1½ cups white sugar
5 tablespoons fish sauce
2 large red chillies, finely sliced on the diagonal
vegetable oil for deep-frying

Wontons

9 uncooked medium-sized prawns
(shrimp) – about 300 g (10 oz)
1 tablespoon roughly chopped coriander
(cilantro) leaves
1 tablespoon finely sliced spring onions
(scallions)
1½ teaspoons finely diced ginger
1 teaspoon shao hsing wine or dry sherry
1 teaspoon light soy sauce
1 teaspoon oyster sauce
¼ teaspoon white sugar
¼ teaspoon sesame oil
16 fresh wonton wrappers,
about 7 cm (3 in) square

Place vinegar and sugar in a medium-sized heavy-based saucepan and bring to the boil. Reduce heat and simmer, uncovered, for about 15 minutes or until liquid is reduced by almost half and slightly syrupy. Remove from stove, stir in fish sauce and chillies and set aside.

For the wontons, peel and de-vein prawns, then dice prawn meat (see pages 124–5) – you should have about 150 g (5 oz) diced prawn meat. Combine prawn meat and remaining ingredients, except wonton wrappers, in a bowl, cover and refrigerate for 30 minutes.

Next, fill and shape the wontons (see pages 266–7).

Heat oil in a hot wok until surface seems to shimmer slightly. Add wontons in batches and deep-fry for about 2 minutes or until just cooked and lightly browned. To test the wontons you will need to remove one using a slotted spoon and cut into it with a sharp knife to see if the prawns are cooked through. Remove wontons with a slotted spoon and drain well on kitchen paper. Repeat process with remaining wontons.

Arrange wontons on a platter and serve immediately with a bowl of sweet chilli dipping sauce.

Prawn Wontons with Sichuan Chilli Oil

Serve as a starter for 4

2 teaspoons dried chilli flakes

½ cup vegetable oil

2 tablespoons light soy sauce

2 tablespoons hot water

1 tablespoon rice wine vinegar

2 teaspoons white sugar

pinch Sichuan pepper and salt
(see page 14)

Wontons

9 uncooked medium-sized prawns
(shrimp) – about 300 g (10 oz)

1 tablespoon roughly chopped
coriander (cilantro) leaves

1 tablespoon finely sliced spring
onions (scallions)

1½ teaspoons finely diced ginger

1 teaspoon shao hsing wine
or dry sherry

1 teaspoon light soy sauce

1 teaspoon oyster sauce

¼ teaspoon white sugar

¼ teaspoon sesame oil

16 fresh wonton wrappers,
about 7 cm (3 in) square

On my last trip to the vibrant city of Hong Kong, I was very taken with a dish I had several times in a little restaurant called Yellow Door. The owner was so kind and took me into the kitchen to show me how it was made. The distinctive Sichuan chilli oil is heavenly – an amazing combination of smoky, mysterious, unusual, spicy, sweet, sour and salty flavours – and is absolutely delicious drizzled over boiled, silky wontons. This recipe makes about ¾ cup chilli oil; if you have any left over, it goes very well with steamed fish fillets or white-cooked chicken.

1 First make the Sichuan chilli oil. Place chilli in a heatproof bowl. Heat oil in a small heavy-based frying pan until the surface shimmers slightly. Carefully pour hot oil over chilli in the bowl to release the heat and flavour. Stir to combine and stand, uncovered, for 30 minutes.

2 Strain cooled oil mixture over a bowl through a fine sieve and discard chilli flakes remaining in sieve. Stir in remaining ingredients, except Sichuan pepper and salt, and set aside.

3 For the wontons, peel and de-vein prawns, then dice prawn meat (see pages 124–5) – you should have about 150 g (5 oz) diced prawn meat. Combine prawn meat and remaining ingredients, except wonton wrappers, in a bowl, cover and refrigerate for 30 minutes.

4 Next fill and shape the wontons (see pages 266–7).

5 Bring a large saucepan of water to the boil. Drop wontons, in batches, into the water and cook for 2 minutes or until wontons are just cooked through. To test the wontons you will need to remove one using a slotted spoon and cut it through with a sharp knife to see if the prawns are just cooked through. Remove wontons with a slotted spoon and drain. Repeat process with remaining wontons.

6 To serve, arrange wontons on a platter. Stir Sichuan chilli oil well to combine before spooning some of the oil over the wontons. Serve immediately sprinkled with Sichuan pepper and salt.

Stir-Fried Hokkien Noodles with Chicken and Oyster Mushrooms

Serve as a meal for 4 or as part of a banquet for 4–6

My mother insists that chicken thigh fillets are better for stir-frying than chicken breast fillets as they remain more moist and tender – and she is right! I like to lightly marinate the chicken before cooking, to give the dish an overall depth of flavour and help to create a lovely, rich sauce.

400 g (13 oz) chicken thigh fillets,
**   cut into 2 cm (1 in) slices**
¼ cup vegetable oil
150 g (5 oz) fresh oyster mushrooms,
**   stems discarded**
1 small red onion, cut in half and then
**   into thick wedges**
4 spring onions (scallions), trimmed
**   and cut into 10 cm (4 in) lengths**
12 ginger slices
1 × 450 g (15 oz) packet fresh Hokkien noodles
2 tablespoons light soy sauce
2 tablespoons shao hsing wine or dry sherry
1 tablespoon white sugar
1 tablespoon malt vinegar
½ teaspoon sesame oil
¼ cup coriander (cilantro) sprigs
2 large red chillies, finely sliced on the diagonal
2 tablespoons light soy sauce, extra

Marinade
1 tablespoon white sugar
1 tablespoon light soy sauce
1 tablespoon shao hsing wine
**   or dry sherry**
½ teaspoon sesame oil

Combine chicken and marinade ingredients in a bowl, cover, and leave to marinate in the refrigerator for 30 minutes.

Heat 2 tablespoons of the oil in a hot wok until surface seems to shimmer slightly. Add chicken and stir-fry for 1 minute. Remove from wok and set aside.

Add remaining oil to hot wok with mushrooms, onion, spring onions and ginger and stir-fry for 1 minute or until onion is lightly browned. Toss in noodles, reserved chicken, soy sauce, wine or sherry, sugar, vinegar and sesame oil and stir-fry for a further 2 minutes or until chicken is just cooked through and noodles are hot.

Arrange noodles in bowls and top with coriander sprigs. Serve immediately with a small bowl of sliced chilli mixed with the extra soy sauce.

Stir-Fried Hokkien Noodles with Chicken, Chilli and Bean Sprouts

Serve as a meal for 4 or as part of a banquet for 4–6

This combination of chicken, chilli and bean sprouts reminds me of the zesty noodle dishes of Thailand. Remember that Hokkien noodles are already cooked when you buy them from the supermarket, so all you are really doing in a stir-fry is heating them through; another reason why the world loves Hokkien noodles – they are so QUICK AND EASY!!!

400 g (13 oz) chicken thigh fillets,
    cut into 2 cm (1 in) slices
¼ cup vegetable oil
1 small white onion, cut in half and
    then into thick wedges
12 ginger slices
1 × 450 g (15 oz) packet fresh Hokkien noodles
2 tablespoons shao hsing wine or dry sherry
1 tablespoon white sugar
1 tablespoon light soy sauce
1 tablespoon oyster sauce
1 tablespoon malt vinegar
½ teaspoon sesame oil
1 cup fresh bean sprouts
½ cup spring onion (scallion) julienne
2 large red chillies, finely sliced on the diagonal

Marinade
1 tablespoon white sugar
1 tablespoon light soy sauce
1 tablespoon shao hsing wine
    or dry sherry
½ teaspoon sesame oil

Combine chicken and marinade ingredients in a bowl, cover, and leave to marinate in the refrigerator for 30 minutes.

Heat 2 tablespoons of the oil in a hot wok until surface seems to shimmer slightly. Add chicken and stir-fry for 1 minute. Remove from wok and set aside.

Add remaining oil to hot wok with onion and ginger and stir-fry for 1 minute or until onion is lightly browned. Toss in noodles, reserved chicken, wine or sherry, sugar, soy sauce, oyster sauce, vinegar and sesame oil and stir-fry for 1½ minutes. Add bean sprouts, spring onion and half the chilli and stir-fry for a further 30 seconds or until chicken is just cooked through and noodles are hot.

Arrange noodles in bowls, top with remaining chilli and serve immediately.

Stir-Fried Hokkien Noodles
with Prawns, Chilli and Bean Sprouts

Serve as a meal for 4 or as part of a banquet for 4–6

It is so simple to lightly sear some peeled prawns and toss them into a Hokkien noodle dish, yet the result is rather exotic. The addition of chilli and bean sprouts adds texture and spice. You could also use fish fillets or squid in this dish.

12 uncooked medium-sized prawns (shrimp) –
   about 400 g (13 oz)
⅓ cup vegetable oil
1 medium-sized red onion, finely sliced
12 ginger slices
3 garlic cloves, finely sliced
1 × 450 g (15 oz) packet fresh Hokkien noodles
2 tablespoons shao hsing wine or dry sherry

2 tablespoons light soy sauce
1 tablespoon malt vinegar
1 teaspoon white sugar
½ teaspoon sesame oil
1 cup fresh bean sprouts
1 cup spring onion (scallion) julienne
1 large red chilli, finely sliced on the diagonal

Peel, de-vein and butterfly prawns (see pages 124–5), leaving tails intact.

Heat half the oil in a hot wok until surface seems to shimmer slightly. Add prawns and sear on each side for 30 seconds or until lightly browned. Remove from wok and set aside.

Add remaining oil to hot wok with onion, ginger and garlic and stir-fry for 1 minute or until onion is lightly browned. Toss in noodles, reserved prawns, wine or sherry, soy sauce, vinegar, sugar and sesame oil and stir-fry for 30 seconds. Finally add bean sprouts, half the spring onion and half the chilli and stir-fry for a further 30 seconds or until prawns are just cooked through and noodles are hot.

Arrange noodles in bowls, top with remaining spring onion and chilli and serve immediately.

Stir-Fried Hokkien Noodles with Sweet Pork Fillets

Serve as a meal for 4 or as part of a banquet for 4–6

Mum and I always marinate pork whenever we stir-fry it, as it tends to be a little dry. I marinate it in hoisin sauce and shao hsing wine or dry sherry, to offset the richness of the pork. Finish the dish with a sprinkle of Sichuan pepper and salt to add that extra Asian touch.

400 g (13 oz) pork fillets, cut into 5 mm (¼ in) slices
½ large red pepper
¼ cup vegetable oil
1 small white onion, cut in half and then into thick wedges
4 spring onions (scallions), trimmed and cut into 10 cm (4 in) lengths
12 ginger slices
3 garlic cloves, finely sliced
1 × 450 g (15 oz) packet fresh Hokkien noodles
2 tablespoons shao hsing wine or dry sherry
1 tablespoon light soy sauce
1 tablespoon oyster sauce
½ teaspoon sesame oil
pinch Sichuan pepper and salt (see page 14)

Marinade
1 tablespoon shao hsing wine or dry sherry
1 tablespoon hoisin sauce
1 tablespoon malt vinegar
1 tablespoon white sugar
2 teaspoons light soy sauce
½ teaspoon sesame oil

Combine pork and marinade ingredients in a bowl, cover, and leave to marinate in the refrigerator for 30 minutes.

Remove seeds and membranes from pepper, cut into fine slices and set aside.

Heat 2 tablespoons of the oil in a hot wok until surface seems to shimmer slightly. Add pork and stir-fry for 1 minute. Remove from wok and set aside.

Add remaining oil to hot wok with pepper, onion, spring onions, ginger and garlic and stir-fry for 1 minute or until onion is lightly browned. Toss in noodles and reserved pork and stir-fry for 30 seconds. Finally, add wine or sherry, soy sauce, oyster sauce and sesame oil and stir-fry for a further 1½ minutes or until pork is cooked through and noodles are hot.

Arrange noodles in bowls, sprinkle with Sichuan pepper and salt and serve immediately.

side dishes and pickles

Hot and Sour Cucumbers

Serve as a side dish to accompany a meal or as part of a banquet for 6–8

These cucumbers make a wonderful accompaniment to a banquet served for a long lunch! Refreshing, salty, sweet, sour and spicy – YUM!!! My kind of food.

4 medium-sized cucumbers, peeled
1 teaspoon white sugar
1 teaspoon sea salt
1 cup white vinegar
¾ cup white sugar, extra
¼ cup fish sauce

1 tablespoon lemon juice
1 large red chilli, finely sliced on the diagonal
1 teaspoon Sichuan pepper and salt
(see page 14)
⅛ teaspoon chilli oil

Cut cucumbers in half lengthways and scoop out the seeds using a spoon. Place cut-side down on a chopping board and slice on the diagonal into 2 cm (1 in) pieces. Combine in a bowl with sugar and salt, mix well and leave to stand for 1 hour.

Meanwhile, combine vinegar and extra sugar in a small heavy-based saucepan and stir over heat until sugar dissolves. Simmer, uncovered and without stirring, for about 8 minutes, or until reduced by one-third and slightly syrupy – you should have about ¾ cup. Set aside to cool.

Drain away any excess liquid from cucumbers. Add cooled vinegar syrup and remaining ingredients to pickled cucumbers and transfer to a serving bowl.

Note: This dish should be served on the day of making.

Goong Goong's Pickles

Serve as a side dish to accompany a meal (makes 2.5 kg/5 lb pickles)

750 g (1 lb 8 oz) cabbage

1 medium-sized cucumber

2 medium-sized carrots, peeled

1 medium-sized white radish
  (daikon), peeled

1 bunch red radishes

¼ cup sea salt

6 cups white vinegar

2¼ cups white sugar

¼ cup light soy sauce

1 teaspoon chilli oil

This recipe came from my mother's father (my grandfather), Goong Goong. These dynamic, delicious pickles remind me a little of Italian giardinera: straight from the jar, they're perfect served as an appetiser or palate awakener, or finely sliced they can be added to a salad or thrown into a stir-fry to add body and complexity.

1 Remove core from cabbage and cut into irregular pieces about 5 x 2 cm (2 x 1 in). Roughly pull pieces apart to separate leaves. Slice cucumber and carrots in half lengthways, then cut into batons about 7 x 1 cm (3 x ½ in). Slice white radish in half lengthways and cut into pieces roughly 3 x 2 cm (1¼ x 1 in). Trim red radishes then cut in half.

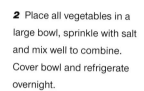

2 Place all vegetables in a large bowl, sprinkle with salt and mix well to combine. Cover bowl and refrigerate overnight.

3 Combine vinegar and sugar in a medium-sized heavy-based saucepan and stir over heat until sugar dissolves. Simmer, uncovered and without stirring, for about 30 minutes, or until reduced by about one-third and slightly syrupy. Set aside to cool then refrigerate overnight.

4 Next day, pour cooled syrup over salted vegetables, add remaining ingredients and mix thoroughly. Transfer to a jar or other airtight container and store in the refrigerator for 2–3 days to allow flavours to develop before using (refrigerated, they will keep for several months).

Sour Chinese Cabbage with Sesame Oil

Serve as a side dish to accompany a meal or as part of a banquet for 6–8

We Chinese just love sour flavours, and this recipe is great in summer or winter as a cheeky little addition to any Chinese banquet – it's complex yet refined at the same time.

½ Chinese cabbage – about 800 g (1 lb 10 oz)
3 teaspoons white sugar
3 teaspoons sea salt
1 cup white vinegar
¾ cup white sugar, extra
¾ cup malt vinegar

¼ cup light soy sauce
2 tablespoons fish sauce
1 teaspoon sesame oil
1 teaspoon Sichuan pepper and salt
(see page 14)

Cut cabbage crossways into 3 cm (1¼ in) pieces. Combine in a bowl with sugar and salt, mix well and leave to stand for 45 minutes.

Meanwhile, combine vinegar and extra sugar in a small heavy-based saucepan and stir over heat until sugar dissolves. Simmer, uncovered and without stirring, for about 8 minutes, or until reduced by one-third and slightly syrupy – you should have about ¾ cup. Set aside to cool.

Add cooled vinegar syrup and remaining ingredients except Sichuan pepper and salt to pickled cabbage and transfer to a serving bowl. Sprinkle with Sichuan pepper and salt and serve.

Note: This dish should be served on the day of making.

Pickled Carrot and Onions

Serve as a side dish to accompany a meal or as part of a banquet for 6–8

Yum, yum, yum – easy, easy, easy!!! These simple pickles are great with meat dishes, fish dishes or just on their own.

4 medium-sized carrots, peeled
1 bunch salad onions, trimmed
3 teaspoons white sugar
3 teaspoons sea salt

1 cup white vinegar
¾ cup white sugar, extra
¼ cup fish sauce
2½ tablespoons lemon juice
1 lemon, halved

Cut carrots in half lengthways and roughly slice on the diagonal. Remove and discard outer layer of onions and roughly slice. Combine carrots and onions in a bowl with sugar and salt, mix well and leave to stand for 2½ hours.

Meanwhile, combine vinegar and extra sugar in a small heavy-based saucepan and stir over heat until sugar dissolves. Simmer, uncovered and without stirring, for about 8 minutes, or until reduced by one-third and slightly syrupy – you should have about ¾ cup. Set aside to cool.

Drain carrot and onion mixture and, using your hands, gently squeeze away any excess liquid.

Add cooled vinegar syrup, fish sauce and lemon juice to pickled vegetables and transfer to a serving bowl, with lemon halves.

Note: This dish should be served on the day of making.

EATING CHINESE-STYLE

Throughout China, the basic notion of a meal is the same. There is always a grain – usually boiled or steamed rice – which is complemented by several dishes made up of different ingredients. Even in the most unassuming home, dinner usually comprises separate meat, seafood and vegetable dishes, as well as soup, rice and tea; a lavish Chinese banquet can include up to 20 or more dishes!

The notion of a 'main' dish as such does not exist in Chinese cooking. A meal will be composed of several dishes, all served at once and designed to be shared communally. This shared style of eating actually makes Chinese cuisine a very healthy choice: you tend to eat a much wider range of foods, with a variety of tastes and textures, and to consume several slivers of meat and fish per meal – always married with vegetables – rather than a large steak or chicken leg, as you might in a Western-style meal. To me, eating Chinese-style makes a lot of sense. I like the 'grazing' style of this eating – it makes for interesting, vibrant eating that is sociable and interactive, and where one mouthful is never the same as the next.

The Chinese table setting is quite simple: each diner has a pair of chopsticks and a three-piece set – a spoon for soup, a bowl for rice and a saucer for discarding fish and chicken bones, and so on. If Chinese tea is served throughout the meal, each diner will also have a tea cup. Chinese table etiquette is informal and relaxed, with the emphasis on contrasting flavours, textures and ingredients, rather than the ritual of eating itself, as in Western table etiquette.

HOW TO USE CHOPSTICKS

I often remark on the fact that tea somehow tastes better when sipped from finely crafted tea cups and saucers. Well, the same is true when it comes to eating Chinese food with chopsticks . . . it just seems to taste better. Chopsticks are not vital to Chinese dining or cooking, but I believe it does add to the whole experience if you get to know how to use them. They are not difficult to master – like all things, practice is the key. At home, I use chopsticks all the time, even when I am eating a Western-style salad! I just love eating small mouthfuls of everything and I love the delicate way chopsticks allow you to handle food.

Chopsticks for everyday use are made of plastic, lacquered wood or plain bamboo. The wooden or bamboo ones are very practical: they are not slippery in hands that are not used to them, and are easy to clean and dry, extremely inexpensive and available everywhere. Most chopsticks are about 25 centimetres (10 inches) long and about the thickness of a pencil; they are square at the top end for holding and pointed at the bottom end for picking up and eating or cooking. My mum and I both have a giant pair of wooden chopsticks, which are approximately 45 centimetres (18 inches) long and are excellent for cooking with – especially for deep-frying, as you can handle the food as it cooks, while keeping a safe distance from the hot oil. Chopsticks are excellent for stir-frying too, as they can swiftly slip around and under pieces of food without disfiguring them.

There are a variety of ways of holding chopsticks for eating – basically it comes down to what works for different people's hands. The basic principle however, remains the same: keep the bottom chopstick *firm*, and allow the top chopstick to *move*. Chopsticks should be held two-thirds of the way up from the pointy ends; don't make the mistake of holding the chopsticks too close to the tips, which reduces manoeuvrability. Both chopsticks are held in one hand but the one stick is held stationary, while the other is moved with a pincer-like action. It is important to keep the tips of the chopsticks level with each other at all times – you can do this by lightly tapping the ends together on the plate.

Chopsticks can pick up any food that is cut into bite-sized pieces, whether it is diced, sliced, slivered or shredded. Larger pieces of food can be broken apart by chopsticks as long as the food is tender, while smooth, finely minced foods are scooped rather than grasped by the chopsticks. Succulent food, such as whole steamed fish, is easily pulled apart with chopsticks; eating fish with chopsticks makes for a very elegant and refined experience, since the chopsticks do not bruise or batter the delicate flesh.

We have all seen and no doubt *heard* the Chinese 'eating rice' with their chopsticks! Holding the bowl in their non-chopstick hand, the chopsticks are used to scoop the rice from bowl to mouth. To get the crucial last few grains, the bowl is brought right up to the mouth in a 'drinking' position, and the rice is shovelled in, rather swiftly – the significance of this is that rice, which is symbolic of blessings in life, must be received in abundance. Each night around the dinner table my father would warn us that if we did not eat all the rice grains in our bowl, we would wake up in the morning with the equivalent number of pimples on our face. Our bowls were always spotless!

1 With your dominant hand (your right, if you're right-handed) in a relaxed, half-open position, place the first chopstick between the tip of your third finger and the base of your thumb. Hold the chopstick firmly, bracing it against the third finger with the middle of your thumb. Keep this chopstick fixed in this position.

2 Place the second chopstick between the tip of your thumb and the tips of your index and middle fingers, holding it lightly.

3 Use your middle finger to move the second chopstick away from the first – this opens the tips of the chopsticks, ready for action!

4 To grasp the food, move the second chopstick back towards the first, again using the middle finger. Then just raise the food to your mouth . . .

MENU PLANNING

Planning a Chinese meal is an art in itself. It calls for the careful selection of individual dishes that all harmonise together and enhance one another. The essence of Chinese cuisine is creating a balance between cooking techniques and ingredient flavours, textures and colours to produce a well-balanced, interesting and well-received meal. Whatever the ingredients, whether lavish or simple, each dish should be stimulating and imaginative. Here are some points to consider:

> Only cook what you love to eat yourself – the results are so much better when we love what we do.

> Do you have little or lots of time to prepare the meal? The degree of involvement, preparation and cooking time should reflect this . . . Try to prevent a stressful situation for yourself by cooking easy dishes during the week, for example, and saving more elaborate dishes for the weekend when you can take your time and enjoy making them.

> What mood are you in? Are you in a 'no-mess, no-fuss but absolutely starving for something delicious mood', or are you in a relaxed, adventurous, flamboyant mood, ready to explore and create?

> What ingredients are in season? I cannot stress this enough. When you buy food that is at the peak of its season, it will be ripe and full of flavour, and the price will be as good as it gets, due to the plentiful supply.

> For inner wellbeing and physical comfort, aim to cook 'cooling' food in the warmer months and 'warming' food in the cooler months.

> On a practical level, be realistic about what you can comfortably manage in your kitchen – think about space, work surfaces, the size of your oven and cooktop, and so on.

> Think about the ages and tastes of the people who'll be eating . . . Are there any vegetarians or people with allergies or food intolerances? Are you feeding big eaters or 'pickers'?

> When planning dinner parties, consider the personalities of your guests, and what they enjoy eating the most. Also try to visualise the table: how everything will fit onto the table; what platter or bowl you'll use to serve each dish; and what dishes work well together.

VIKING STUDIO
Published by the Penguin Group
Penguin Group (USA) Inc., 375 Hudson Street,
New York, New York 10014, U.S.A.
Penguin Group (Canada), 90 Eglinton Avenue East, Suite 700,
Toronto, Ontario, Canada M4P 2Y3
(a division of Pearson Penguin Canada Inc.)
Penguin Books Ltd, 80 Strand, London WC2R 0RL., England
Penguin Ireland, 25 St. Stephen's Green, Dublin 2, Ireland
(a division of Penguin Books Ltd)
Penguin Books Australia Ltd, 250 Camberwell Road, Camberwell,
Victoria 3124, Australia
(a division of Pearson Australia Group Pty Ltd)
Penguin Books India Pvt Ltd, 11 Community Centre, Panchsheel Park,
New Delhi – 110 017, India
Penguin Group (NZ), Cnr Airborne and Rosedale Roads, Albany,
Auckland 1310, New Zealand
(a division of Pearson New Zealand Ltd)
Penguin Books (South Africa) (Pty) Ltd, 24 Sturdee Avenue,
Rosebank, Johannesburg 2196, South Africa

Penguin Books Ltd, Registered Offices:
80 Strand, London WC2R 0RL, England

First American edition
Published in 2007 by Viking Studio,
a member of Penguin Group (USA) Inc.

10 9 8 7 6 5 4 3 2 1

Text copyright © Kylie Kwong
Photographs copyright © Earl Carter, 2006
All rights reserved

ISBN 978-0-670-03848-0

Printed in the United Kingdom by Butler and Tanner Ltd, Frome
Set in Apollo MT, Nimbus Novus, and Avenir
Design by Tony Palmer © Penguin Group (Australia)